PREFACE

This manual of basic descriptive statistics is designed to serve two purposes: (1) to assist the student in understanding the statistics necessary for constructing better teacher-made tests and in interpreting the test manuals accompanying standardized tests and (2) to introduce some basic statistical concepts for the behavioral sciences student in the most painless way possible. The emphasis is on understanding statistical techniques rather than on mathematical derivation of formulas, so no prerequisites other than ninth-grade algebra are assumed.

Many college instructors of tests and measurements feel that no single text is sufficient for their purpose; rather, they prefer to use several texts as reference material. This manual is designed with this in mind, and is intended to provide the basic foundation in statistics that is required for an understanding of tests and measurements. And in courses where a single text is used, this manual can serve as a valuable supplement to the chapters on statistics. Properly used, the manual can save much class time that is usually expended in explanations and calculations. The table of cross-references on page viii shows how the chapters of this manual correspond to the sections of a number of current tests-and-measurements texts.

Each chapter has a number of illustrative examples with full explanations of the calculations involved. It will be to the student's advantage to follow the steps closely and then go on directly to the problems at the end of each chapter. These examples and extra problems, plus the step-by-step explanation and possible interpretations for each statistical concept, should give the student adequate proficiency in each area of measurement.

Grouped data techniques have been included for the mean, median, and standard deviation for the convenience of those who wish to calculate these statistics for data that have been grouped into a frequency distribution. It is up to the discretion of the individual instructor as to whether or not these techniques should be included.

Because of the introductory nature of this manual, a number of statistical procedures have been omitted. The student is referred to a current statistics or tests-and-measurements text for techniques beyond the intended scope of this manual. Basic Statistical Concepts in Education and the Behavioral Sciences by this author and publisher is especially recommended.

In order to make the illustrative examples in this manual easy to calculate, the computations are based on a small number of scores. The conclusions drawn from these examples assume that the number of scores would be considerably greater. The same restriction applies to the problems at the end of each chapter.

I want to thank the many users of past editions of this manual for their suggestions which have been incorporated in this edition. I am especially grateful to Albert Baxter, Joseph Currier, Albert Krueger, and Gene Nichols for their suggestions and criticisms, and to Dr. Helen Wilson of Eastern Montana College for her thorough review of the manuscript and her many helpful comments. Finally, I owe a special note of thanks to my wife, Sol, for manuscript typing and assistance in editing.

Albert E. Bartz

Moorhead, Minnesota

FIFTH EDITION

DESCRIPTIVE STATISTICS

for Education and the Behavioral Sciences

ALBERT E. BARTZ
Concordia College
Moorhead, Minnesota

Burgess Publishing Company
Minneapolis, Minnesota

Copyright © 1979, 1971, 1966, 1963, 1958 by **Albert E. Bartz**
Library of Congress Catalog Card Number 77-91504
ISBN 0-8087-2053-9
Printed in the United States of America.

All rights reserved. No part of this book may be reproduced in any form whatsoever, by photograph or mimeograph or by any other means, by broadcast or transmission, by translation into any kind of language, nor by recording electronically or otherwise, without permission in writing from the publisher, except by a reviewer, who may quote brief passages in critical articles and reviews.

0 9 8 7 6 5 4 3 2 1

CONTENTS

1 Measurement and Scales 1
2 Frequency Distributions 5
3 Measures of Central Tendency 27
4 Percentiles and Norms 49
5 Measures of Variability 59
6 Correlation 79
7 Evaluation and Interpretation of Tests 97

    Appendix I: Answers to Problems 117
    Appendix II: Table of Squares and Square Roots 121
    Index 131

A cross-reference chart correlating *Descriptive Statistics for Education and the Behavioral Sciences* with the most widely used current tests-and-measurements textbooks will be found on pages viii-ix.

FIGURES

1	Histogram of English Scores.	9
2	Frequency Polygon of English Scores	11
3	Theoretical Normal Curve of Distribution.	12
4	Negative Skewness to the Left	13
5	Positive Skewness to the Right	13
6	Negatively Skewed Mathematics Achievement Scores	14
7	Positively Skewed Annual Income Distribution of 12,000 Families . . .	15
8	Normal Curve Showing Mean and SD Distances	65
9	Distribution Curve Showing Mean and SD Units	66
10	Comparison of Two Standard Scores	67
11	Normal Curve and Derived Scales	68
12	Scattergram of Heights and Weights.	82

TABLES

1	Achievement Scores on an English Examination	5
2	Illustration of a Grouped Frequency Distribution	6
3	A Better Illustration of the Grouped Frequency Distribution for the English Achievement Scores	7
4	Simple Frequency Distribution	8
5	Calculation of the Mean	28
6	Raw Scores Expressed as Deviation Scores	29
7	Calculation of the Mode	30
8	Calculation of the Median, N is Odd	31
9	Calculation of the Median, N is Even	32
10	Comparison of the Three Measures of Central Tendency	34
11	Calculation of the Mean for Biology Scores, Grouped Data	36
12	Calculation of the Median for Geography Quiz Scores, Grouped Data	37
13	Age-Grade Equivalents on an Arithmetic Achievement Test	50
14	Percentiles on a College Entrance Examination	52
15	Calculation of Percentiles, Grouped Data	53
16	Two Distributions with Equal Means but Different Ranges	60
17	Two Distributions with Equal Ranges but Dissimilar Patterns of Dispersion	61
18	Calculation of Standard Deviation (Deviation Method)	62
19	Calculation of Standard Deviation (Whole Score Method)	63
20	Comparison of SDs for Two Distributions	64
21	Calculation of the SD for Biology Scores, Grouped Data	69
22	Illustration of Perfect Positive Correlation	79
23	Illustration of Perfect Negative Correlation	80
24	Weights and Heights of 20 College Students	82
25	Illustration of Rank-Difference Method	84
26	Illustration of Pearson Product-Moment r	86
27	Illustration of Odd-Even Method for Determining Reliability	100
28	Calculation of a Validity Coefficient	105

CROSS-REFERENCE CORRELATING
Descriptive Statistics for Education and the Behavioral Sciences
WITH THE MOST WIDELY USED CURRENT TESTS-AND-MEASUREMENTS TEXTBOOKS

Current Textbooks	1	2
Adams and Torgeson, *Measurement and Evaluation in Education, Psychology, and Guidance,* Holt, Rinehart & Winston.		24-26
Ahmann and Glock, *Evaluating Pupil Growth* (4th ed.), Allyn & Bacon.	242-246	247-249
Anastasi, *Psychological Testing* (4th ed.), Macmillan Company.		68-70
Cronbach, *Essentials of Psychological Testing* (3rd ed.), Harper & Row Publishers.		
Ebel, *Essentials of Educational Measurement,* Prentice Hall.		274-276
Garrett, *Testing for Teachers* (2nd ed.), Van Nostrand Reinhold Company.		15-20 258-261
Gronlund, *Measurement and Evaluation in Teaching* (2nd ed.), Macmillan Company.		496-497 501-504
Horrocks and Schoonover, *Measurement for Teachers,* Charles E. Merrill Publishing Company.		38-44 48-50
Noll and Scannel, *Introduction to Educational Measurement* (3rd ed.), Houghton Mifflin Company.	7-13	46-55 71-74
Nunnally, *Educational Measurement and Evaluation* (2nd ed.), McGraw-Hill Book Company.		50-55 58-59
Sax, *Principles of Educational Measurement and Evaluation,* Wadsworth Publishing Company.	136-140	140-141
Scannel and Tracy, *Testing and Measurement in the Classroom,* Houghton Mifflin Company.		182-186
Stanley, *Measurement in Today's Schools* (4th ed.), Prentice-Hall.		54-62 121-124
Thorndike and Hagen, *Measurement and Evaluation in Psychology and Education* (3rd ed.), John Wiley & Sons.		136-140

Chapters in *Descriptive Statistics for Education and the Behavioral Sciences*				
3	4	5	6	7
24-28	28-33 50-56	21-24	74-82	85-92 114-128
249 573-575	252-259 264-272 582-584	245-252 259-264 575-578	288-291 578-581	276-301 303-323
70-72	73-80	72-73 80-84	104-108	27-30 110-133 134-161
	89-94 98	94-102	128-135	121-128 155-171
276-278	285-293 481-484	279-285 485-488	296-303	407-424 435-448
20-21 262-266	26-28 33-37 42-43	22-26 37-41 266-269	28-29 270-271	29-33 240-242
497-499 504-509	370-385	385-390 499-501 504-509	82-84 509-512	77-97 100-112
45-47	50-56	47-48 56-58		65-74
55-61	48-49 97-102 113-121	61-71 75-80 102-107	80-92	135-152
40-45	60-72	46-49 55-58	80-90	106-114
141-147	157-158	147-156	160-168	172-196 206-225
186-188	193-195	188-193	196-199	199-214
63-73	66-69 132-135	73-81 139-143	86-101	151-164
140-146	143 210-224	146-154 224-229	154-158	163-195

Numbers refer to current textbook pages that match each chapter of this book.

Chapter 1

MEASUREMENT AND SCALES

The primary objective of the statistical method is to attach some sort of meaning to a mass of data. This mass of data might be a collection of scores on a history test, or a group of IQ scores taken from cumulative records, or a list of heights and weights of a group of sixth-grade schoolchildren. The task of the statistical method is to reduce the data (thus the term *data reduction*) to some meaningful measures that tell us something about the group of measurements before us.

These measurements, of course, consist of numbers of some kind or another, and we feel very familiar with our number system. After all, we have been adding and subtracting and multiplying and dividing numbers ever since our early elementary school years. But before performing these same arithmetic manipulations on numbers that represent something (test scores, IQ's, heights and weights), we have to be aware of the properties that the numbers have. We cannot blindly manipulate a set of numbers without knowing something about their properties and what they represent. For example, the number 9 representing the hardness of a rock sample is different from a glove size of 9 or 9 items correct on a short geography quiz. The old adage that you cannot add apples and oranges was never more true than in the field of measurement. We must be sensitive to what the numbers represent.

The term *measurement* can be defined as the assignment of numbers to objects or events according to certain prescribed rules. After this has been done, the numbers have certain properties that we must take into account as we perform our arithmetic operations. We can treat these numbers with varying levels of precision, depending upon what they represent. And the easiest way of looking at the "what" of what they represent is to examine four kinds of scales that describe the various levels of measurement. Each type of scale represents a way of assigning numbers to objects or events, and the description of each type shows the rules that were applied.

NOMINAL SCALE

The simplest and most elementary type of measurement is the *nominal* scale. Here numbers are assigned for the sole purpose of differentiating one object from another. Pete has book locker 80, Joe's basketball jersey is number 12, and Ron took a trip on U.S. Highway 81. The nominal scale has the characteristic "different from," and numbers in this scale have only the property of differentiating one thing from another.

In fact, it would not be necessary to use numbers at all to differentiate the categories. We could just as easily use letters of the alphabet, nouns, or proper names. When we categorize groups as male/female, or freshman/sophomore/junior/senior, for example, we are categorizing according to a nominal scale.

When numbers are used in a nominal scale, we would not dream of adding them together or of trying to calculate an average, because this scale does not have the necessary properties to enable us to do so. Book locker 80 is not twice as large as number 40, and Joe is not half as good a basketball player as someone with jersey number 24! But crude as it may be, this scale is still a form of measurement. It has enabled us to discriminate one object or event from another.

ORDINAL SCALE

As the term implies, measurements in an *ordinal* scale have the property of order. The nominal scale above had the property of "different from," but the ordinal scale has the additional property of the "direction of the difference." We now can make statements such as "more than" or "less than," since our measuring system has the property of order. The *ranking* of objects or events would be a good example of an ordinal scale. If Ann, Beth, and Cindy rank 1, 2, and 3 in height in their third-grade class, we know that Ann is taller than Beth, and Beth is taller than Cindy. This is an improvement over the nominal scale, where no indication of the direction of the difference could be made. But note that our scale still does not permit us to say how much different two or more objects or events are. Ann may be 2 inches taller than Beth, who in turn may be 1 inch taller than Cindy, but our measuring system of 1, 2, and 3 applied to their rank in height cannot tell us this.

INTERVAL SCALE

The most important characteristic of the *interval* scale is equality of units. This means that there are equal distances between observation points on the scale. Not only can we specify the direction of the difference but we can now say *how much* of a difference there is. In the height example above, our measuring system now would show that Ann is 49 inches tall, Beth is 47 inches, and Cindy is 46 inches. The difference between Ann and Beth is 2 inches and this is twice as much of a difference as there is between Beth and Cindy. And if another child is 45 inches tall, we would be able to say that the difference between her and Beth is the same as the difference in height between Beth and Ann. With equality of units we can make statements such as this that are meaningful. Probably most measurements that we will be dealing with are of the interval type. Test scores (in terms of number of items correct) are interval measurements.

RATIO SCALE

The *ratio* scale has all the characteristics of the interval scale plus an *absolute zero*. With an absolute zero point we can make statements involving ratios, such as "twice as long" or "half as fast." If John runs the mile in 5 minutes but it takes Pete 10 minutes, we know that John is twice as fast. But in intelligence testing we know that a person with an IQ of 100 is *not* twice as intelligent as someone with an IQ of 50. This is because zero intelligence cannot be defined, and thus there is no absolute zero point. Most physical scales such as length, time, and weight are ratio scales, but very few behavioral measures are of this type.

COMPARING THE FOUR SCALES

Many of the measurements that are made in psychology and education are *performance* measurements, where we infer the amount of the underlying trait instead of measuring the characteristic directly as we do in the physical sciences. It is easy to get the impression that the ideal measurement would be a ratio measurement and that the other three scales are something to be avoided if at all possible. While this may be the theoretical goal of measurement, we are faced with the fact that many behavioral measures miss this ideal by a significant amount, and practical considerations require our making the most of the precision that we do have. It turns out that we can utilize the ordinal and interval scales to a very great degree and obtain some very valuable information from them.

In the chapters to follow, a number of statistics (percentiles, averages, etc.) are discussed and you will very soon realize that a lot of information can be gotten from measurements that do not meet the theoretical ideal of a ratio scale. The important point is that you should be aware of what sort of scale a given body of measurements represents and use the statistical procedures that are appropriate for that scale. After you have done this, the statistics that you do obtain can give a wealth of meaning about a given set of measurements.

Chapter 2
FREQUENCY DISTRIBUTIONS

As we noted in the preceding chapter, the primary objective of the statistical method is to attach some meaning to a group of data. We might be faced with a column of numbers that represent test scores, ages, heights, weights, or almost anything that can be measured. It is our job to reduce this data to meaningful measures that give us some information about the mass of numbers in front of us. Let us consider an example to illustrate how the *frequency distribution* can be one technique that will accomplish this task.

In Table 1 are 50 scores made by students on a classroom test in English.

Table 1

ACHIEVEMENT SCORES ON AN
ENGLISH EXAMINATION

69	70	72	62	78
71	85	72	73	91
71	61	85	82	82
82	81	74	79	90
66	88	82	86	83
89	94	86	76	75
81	79	93	76	80
68	81	64	87	80
95	75	84	90	92
88	97	86	68	67

Notice how difficult it is to get any meaning out of this collection of scores. With some effort we can find the highest score, 97, or the lowest score, 61. We would be hard pressed to find out where the concentrations of scores were, or how many students scored above 85, or how many people had a score of 82. In short, this collection of data gives us very little information about the performance of the group on the English test.

One way to give a little more order to our data would be to arrange the scores in order from highest to lowest. This would immediately give us the highest and lowest scores, of course, and we would be able to tell something about the concentrations at different points in the distribution. However, this is rather time-consuming, and constructing a frequency distribution by grouping our data would be much more efficient.

GROUPED FREQUENCY DISTRIBUTIONS

To construct a grouped frequency distribution, we group our data into intervals by choosing some convenient interval, such as 5 or 10, and tally the number of scores that fall in each interval. For the first step we note the highest and lowest scores—in this case 97 and 61—and make sure that our top and bottom intervals contain these two extreme scores. If we decide to use an interval size of 10, we finish up with only four such intervals. These are shown in the left-hand column of Table 2.

Table 2

ILLUSTRATION OF A GROUPED FREQUENCY DISTRIBUTION

Interval	Tally	Frequency
90-99	ﬀﬀ ///	8
80-89	ﬀﬀ ﬀﬀ ﬀﬀ ﬀﬀ	20
70-79	ﬀﬀ ﬀﬀ ////	14
60-69	ﬀﬀ ///	8
		N = 50

Notice that each interval contains 10 different score values, and not 9 as it would first appear. For example, the interval 90-99 would contain scores of 90-91-92-93-94-95-96-97-98 and 99, or 10 different score values.

Frequency, listed at the top of the right-hand column in Table 2, refers to the number of scores falling in a given interval. For example, eight students had English test scores from 90 to 99. To obtain the frequency in each interval we go through the set of scores one by one and place a tally mark by the interval in which each score lies. The frequency column simply shows the sums of tally marks for each interval.

Unfortunately, Table 2 has only four intervals, and for our purposes this grouping has resulted in a frequency distribution that does not tell us very much about our English scores. It would be better to refine our table by using more and smaller intervals. The size of the interval that we choose is pretty arbitrary; our main interest is in arriving at a frequency distribution that has enough intervals to give us a good idea of where the scores fall.

Let us choose eight intervals with a size of 5. This would give us the frequency distribution shown in Table 3.

Notice that with this refinement we can get a better idea of the spread and concentration of our scores. There is no set rule regarding the number of intervals to use to give the best display of information, but a convenient first approximation is to plan on using from 8 to 15 intervals. We must remember in choosing our intervals that the top interval must contain the highest score, and the bottom interval the lowest score.

Table 3

A BETTER ILLUSTRATION OF THE GROUPED FREQUENCY DISTRIBUTION FOR THE ENGLISH ACHIEVEMENT SCORES

Interval	Tally	Frequency
95-99	//	2
90-94	||||/ /	6
85-89	||||/ ///	8
80-84	||||/ ||||/ //	12
75-79	||||/ //	7
70-74	||||/ //	7
65-69	||||/	5
60-64	///	3
		N = 50

N in Table 3, refers to the number of students in the group measured or to the number of measurements represented by the group scores. We can check the accuracy of our tabulation by comparing the total tally marks for frequency with the number of measurements in our original data. Naturally, this will give us a check only on the total number, not on whether we have the tally marks placed in the correct interval.

One last word on the construction of frequency distributions. It is sometimes helpful, especially in assigning grades, to construct a frequency distribution where the size of the interval is 1. This is called a *simple frequency distribution*, and one has been constructed in Table 4 for the English test scores.

It is obvious that a simple frequency distribution of test scores, which is constructed by tallying as you go through a stack of test papers, could be of great assistance in assigning letter grades on the familiar "curve." For a discussion of the normal curve, see Chapter 5 on measures of variability.

GRAPHING THE FREQUENCY DISTRIBUTION

The Histogram

By inspecting the frequency distribution of Table 3, we can find a certain degree of orderliness in our data. We can see that a few people made low scores and a few made high scores, but the majority of the scores are concentrated toward the middle of the distribution. However, it is still difficult to picture the entire distribution as a whole. Also, certain irregularities in the distribution may escape a casual glance. These difficulties can be overcome by constructing a graph of our scores.

Table 4

SIMPLE FREQUENCY DISTRIBUTION

Score	f	Score	f
97	/	78	/
96		77	
95	/	76	//
94	/	75	//
93	/	74	/
92	/	73	/
91	/	72	//
90	//	71	//
89	/	70	/
88	//	69	/
87	/	68	//
86	///	67	/
85	//	66	/
84	/	65	
83	/	64	/
82	////	63	
81	///	62	/
80	//	61	/
79	//		

Frequency Distributions

One type of graph is called a *histogram.* It is similar to the bar graph that we are familiar with and can be interpreted in much the same way. Figure 1 below shows a histogram for the English test scores based on the frequency distribution of Table 3.

When we examine the histogram of Figure 1, we see that it is not symmetrical and that the shape is irregular. However, there is a tendency for many scores to fall towards the center of the distribution, with progressively fewer scores as you move in either direction from the "hump." We see, also, that there is a wide variation in the scores.

The steps in the construction of a histogram are as follows:

1. Lay out an area on a piece of graph paper that corresponds roughly to the size and proportions of Figure 1. It is a good practice to have the height of the graph about three-fourths of the width. The horizontal line, called the x-axis, is drawn long enough to include all of the scores plus a little unused space at each end. Label this line (*Scores* in this case) and indicate the lower unit of each interval by the appropriate scores.
2. At the left end of the x-axis draw a vertical line called the y-axis. Divide the y-axis into units so that the greatest frequency will not quite reach the

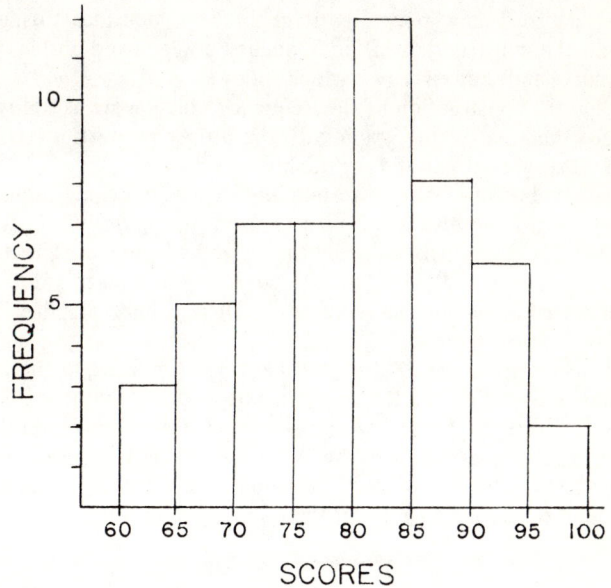

Figure 1

HISTOGRAM OF ENGLISH SCORES

top of the graph. Number these units and label this axis (*Frequency* in this case).
3. Now you can complete the histogram by simply drawing lines parallel to the x-axis at the height represented by the frequency for each interval, and connecting the lines to the x-axis by vertical lines to the lower limits of the intervals. For example, in Figure 1, three people scored in the 60-64 interval, so the horizontal line above the 60-64 interval is drawn three units up from the x-axis, and a vertical line extends down to the lower limit, 60.
4. Give the histogram a title, either above or below the figure. The title should be a clear statement of what the histogram represents.

The Frequency Polygon

Probably most pictorial representations of the frequency distribution take the form of the *frequency polygon,* which is a line graph instead of the bar graph of the histogram. The frequency polygon of the English test scores of Table 3 is shown in Figure 2.

We get the same information from the frequency polygon as we did from the histogram, that is, the concentrations and spread of the scores. Since most graphs of the frequency distribution (including the normal curve to be introduced later) are frequency polygons, it might be a good idea to spend a little extra time on the construction of the frequency polygon and on the material on the normal curve and skewed curves which follows.

The steps in the construction of the frequency polygon are as follows:
1. Lay out the area for the graph with the proper proportions and label the x and y axes just as you did for the histogram.
2. Instead of drawing a bar corresponding to the frequency in each interval as you did for the histogram, place a *dot* at the *midpoint* of each interval. For example, three persons scored in the 60-64 interval. The midpoint of this interval is 62 (60-61-*62*-63-64), so you would place a dot opposite a frequency of 3 and above a score of 62. Then, connect the dots by straight lines.
3. It is incorrect to leave the polygon hanging in mid-air, so the lines at the extreme ends are connected to the x-axis at the midpoint of the adjacent interval, whose frequency, of course, is zero. For example, on the left side of Figure 2 a line connects the point at 62 (the midpoint of the 60-64 interval) with the x-axis at 57 (the midpoint of the interval 55-59). The same method is used to connect the point at 97 with the x-axis at 102.

THE NORMAL CURVE OF DISTRIBUTION

Everyone has heard of, and probably used, the term *normal curve.* Just about all physiological measurements (height, weight, length of nose, number of eye-

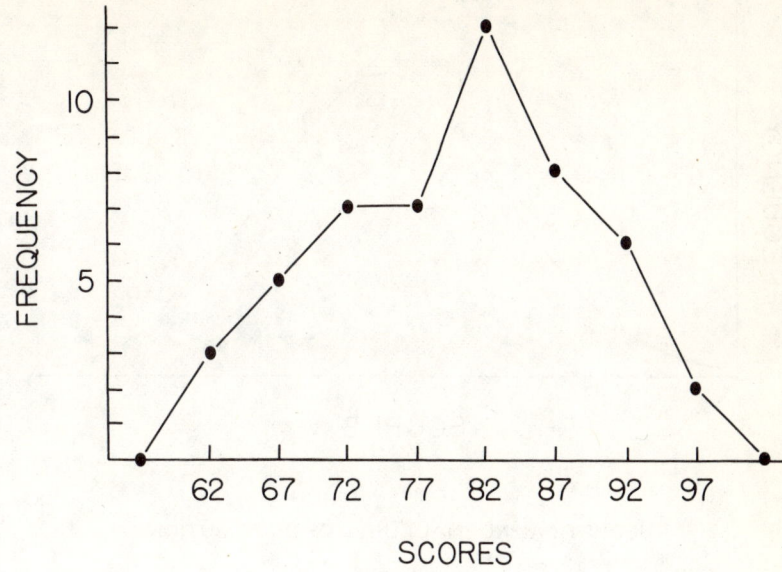

Figure 2

FREQUENCY POLYGON OF ENGLISH SCORES

lashes) and psychological measurements (IQ scores, reaction time, aptitudes) are normally distributed in the population. The normal curve shown in Figure 3 represents what we would expect if we measured some physiological or psychological trait for a *large* number of people in the general population. This symmetrical, bell-shaped frequency polygon shows the typical concentration of scores in the middle of the distribution, with fewer and fewer observations as you approach the extremes. If this were a distribution curve of the heights of American adult males, the curve would be highest (greatest frequency) around 5 feet 9 inches or 5 feet 10 inches and would get progressively lower (smaller and smaller frequency) as you got out towards 6 feet 7 inches or 5 feet 1 inch.

The frequency polygon of the English test scores shown in Figure 2 bears only a small resemblance to the normal curve. When we have only 50 scores, we must expect a lack of symmetry in the distribution. If we had given the English test to 500 students, some of the irregularities would smooth out. And again, if we had a thousand scores, a still more symmetrical distribution would occur.

A perfect normal curve is never attained in actual practice, although there may be some close approximations to it. However, it has some properties that will be useful if our data approximate the normal curve, and we will discuss these properties in a later chapter.

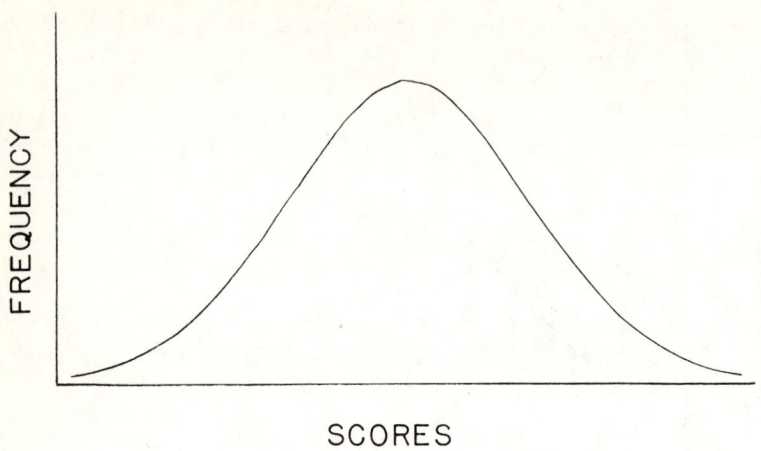

Figure 3

THEORETICAL NORMAL CURVE OF DISTRIBUTION

SKEWNESS

There will be times when a graph of the frequency distribution will not show the typical normal distribution with the majority of the scores concentrated in the center of the distribution. Occasionally you will find that the majority of the scores are at the lower end or the upper end of the distribution. This concentration of scores at one end or the other of the distribution is called *skewness*.

If the scores are heavily concentrated toward the *upper* end of the distribution, we say that the curve is *negatively skewed,* as in Figure 4. As you can see, there is a large concentration of high scores with progressively fewer low scores as you go to the left. Such a distribution might be due to a test being too easy for a particular group of students, with a resulting preponderance of high scores.

If the scores are heavily clustered at the *lower* end of the distribution, we say that the curve is *positively skewed,* as in Figure 5. Here you will notice that there is a large number of low scores with progressively fewer high scores as you go to the right. This type of skewness could be due to a test being too difficult for a particular group, resulting in a large number of low scores.

If you have trouble remembering which type of skewness is which, look for the location of the "tail" of the distribution. If the tail points to the left, as it does in Figure 4, the skewness is negative. If it points to the right, as in Figure 5, the skewness is positive.

If we examine the frequency polygon of the English test scores in Figure 2, we see that there is a very slight negative skewness, since there are a few more scores near the upper end of the scale. This type of skewness is quite common in academic situations, especially in college classes. Since most college classes represent quite a high level of ability, there usually will be more higher scores than lower scores. To put it another way, there usually are more A and B letter grades than D and F grades.

Figures 6 and 7 show examples of negatively and positively skewed curves. Figure 6 shows the results of a national achievement exam in mathematics given in a school system to all ninth-graders enrolled in accelerated classes in mathematics. As you can see, there is a large concentration of high scores with progressively fewer low scores as you go to the left.

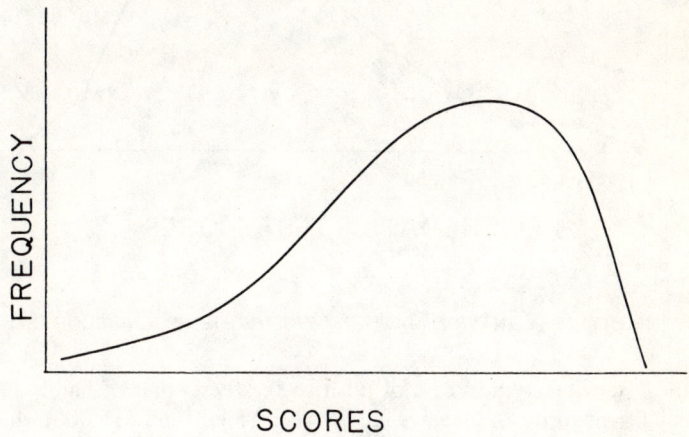

Figure 4

NEGATIVE SKEWNESS TO THE LEFT

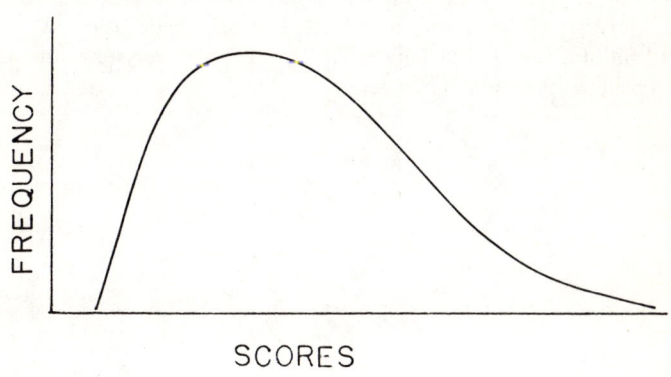

Figure 5

POSITIVE SKEWNESS TO THE RIGHT

14   **Frequency Distributions**

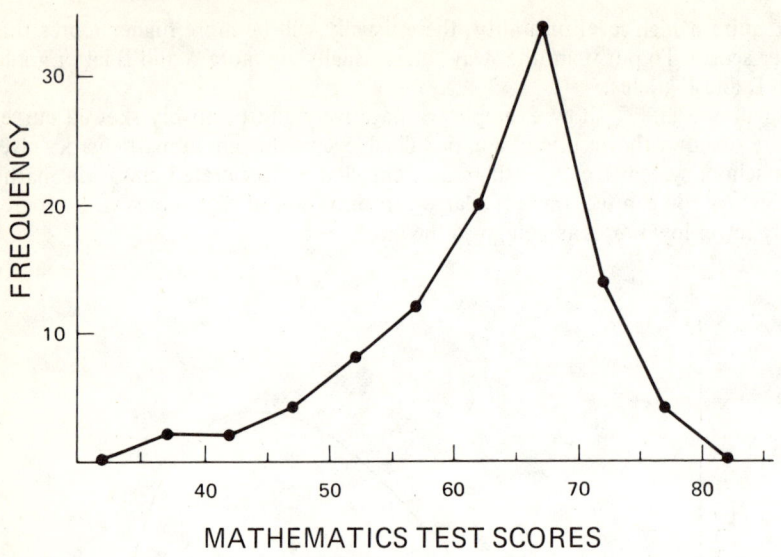

Figure 6

NEGATIVELY SKEWED MATHEMATICS ACHIEVEMENT SCORES

Figure 7 shows a typical case of positive skewness—that of family incomes. Note that the majority of incomes fall between $5,000 and $15,000, which is at the low end of the distribution, while other incomes extend a considerable distance to the right.

Skewness may also be caused by an artificial "floor" or "ceiling" on the measurements in a distribution. For example, the distribution of ages of students at a particular college will be positively skewed, since an artificial floor of age at high-school graduation is the lowest value in the distribution. As a result, the majority of students will be between 18 and 22, with very few younger than 18, but a considerable number older than 22.

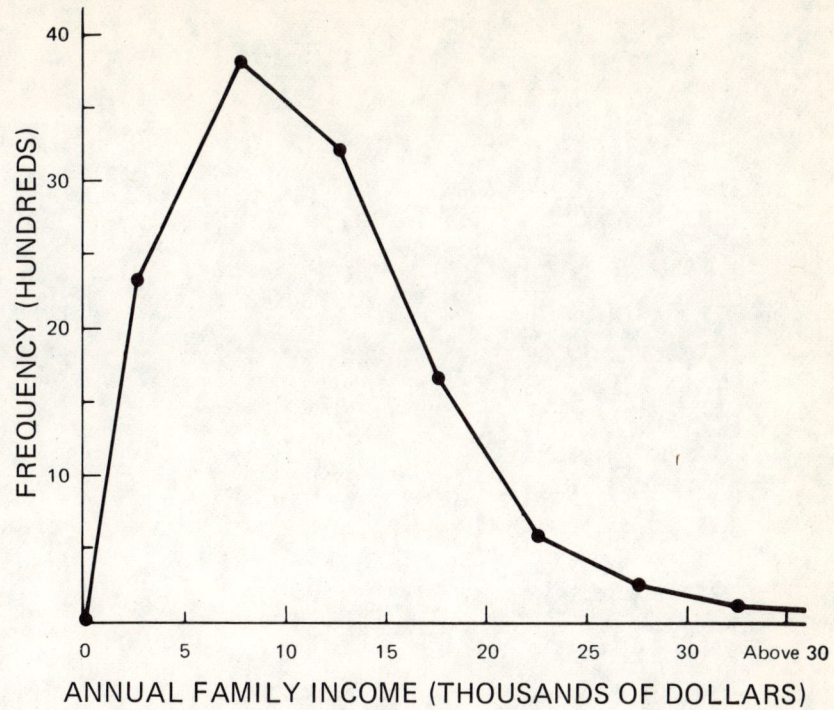

Figure 7

POSITIVELY SKEWED ANNUAL INCOME DISTRIBUTION OF 12,000 FAMILIES

PROBLEMS

1. The data shown below are the results of an exam given to 100 home economics students.

47	49	52	40	48	47	37	47	46	45
35	32	25	35	41	40	30	26	27	42
37	36	36	32	41	42	20	31	29	28
32	37	37	42	27	21	43	22	32	20
38	39	43	38	29	34	16	44	34	33
29	44	30	31	39	32	30	33	23	34
42	24	22	33	28	35	23	31	24	22
25	26	32	27	16	22	36	17	32	34
28	31	23	15	21	17	19	37	14	39
30	27	26	25	16	18	12	13	38	33

From these scores, construct *three* frequency distributions as in Table 3 of the text.

a. Use five intervals, with the bottom interval 10-19 and the top one 50-59.

b. Use nine intervals, with the bottom interval 10-14 and the top one 50-54.

c. Use 15 intervals, with the bottom interval 10-12 and the top one 52-54.

Study the three distributions. Notice the loss of sensitivity when there are only 5 intervals. Also observe the distribution when there are 15. Notice that there is a loss of sensitivity when too many intervals are used. A rule of thumb which is often helpful is to use from 8 to 15 intervals, depending upon the number and the range of the scores.

2. The following scores on a driver-education examination were made by 60 high-school sophomores.

81	60	71	46	62	57	65	54	47	59
56	43	53	67	63	60	61	62	72	83
80	70	64	78	63	68	68	43	58	52
77	60	62	47	59	61	66	55	51	53
79	70	61	73	55	69	65	50	56	44
57	49	52	66	64	63	58	64	74	75

a. Construct a frequency distribution using nine intervals, with the bottom interval 40-44 and the top one 80-84.

Frequency Distributions

b. Use graph paper to construct a frequency polygon for this distribution. Note that you can get a clear picture of the concentration about the center and the small number of scores at the extreme ends of the distribution.

3. A college entrance examination is given to 110 students with the following results.

54	23	12	10	18	5	17	47	47	45
44	52	51	49	8	48	47	43	42	42
41	44	44	43	49	43	43	38	38	38
37	40	39	39	43	39	38	36	35	35
35	37	37	36	36	36	36	33	33	32
32	34	32	34	33	33	33	31	31	31
31	32	30	32	30	32	31	30	29	29
29	31	29	30	28	30	30	28	28	28
27	29	27	28	26	28	28	25	25	24
24	27	13	27	23	26	26	21	21	20
19	19	18	23	18	23	22	17	16	14

a. From this data construct a frequency distribution using some appropriate interval size.

b. Use graph paper to construct a histogram for this data.

4. A national test is given to 120 students in accelerated classes in eleventh-grade English.

74	66	64	61	60	58	56	55	52	50	48	44
73	66	63	61	59	58	56	55	52	50	48	43
72	66	62	61	59	58	56	54	51	50	48	43
69	65	62	61	59	58	55	54	51	50	47	42
68	65	62	61	59	57	55	53	51	49	47	40
68	65	62	61	59	57	55	53	51	49	47	39
68	65	61	61	59	57	55	53	51	49	46	39
67	64	61	60	59	57	55	52	51	49	46	38
67	64	61	60	59	56	55	52	51	48	45	37
66	64	61	60	59	56	55	52	50	48	44	34

Frequency Distributions

a. Construct a frequency distribution and draw a frequency polygon (use graph paper) for this distribution.

b. Inspect the frequency polygon. What kind of skewness has occurred? What would be the reason for this result?

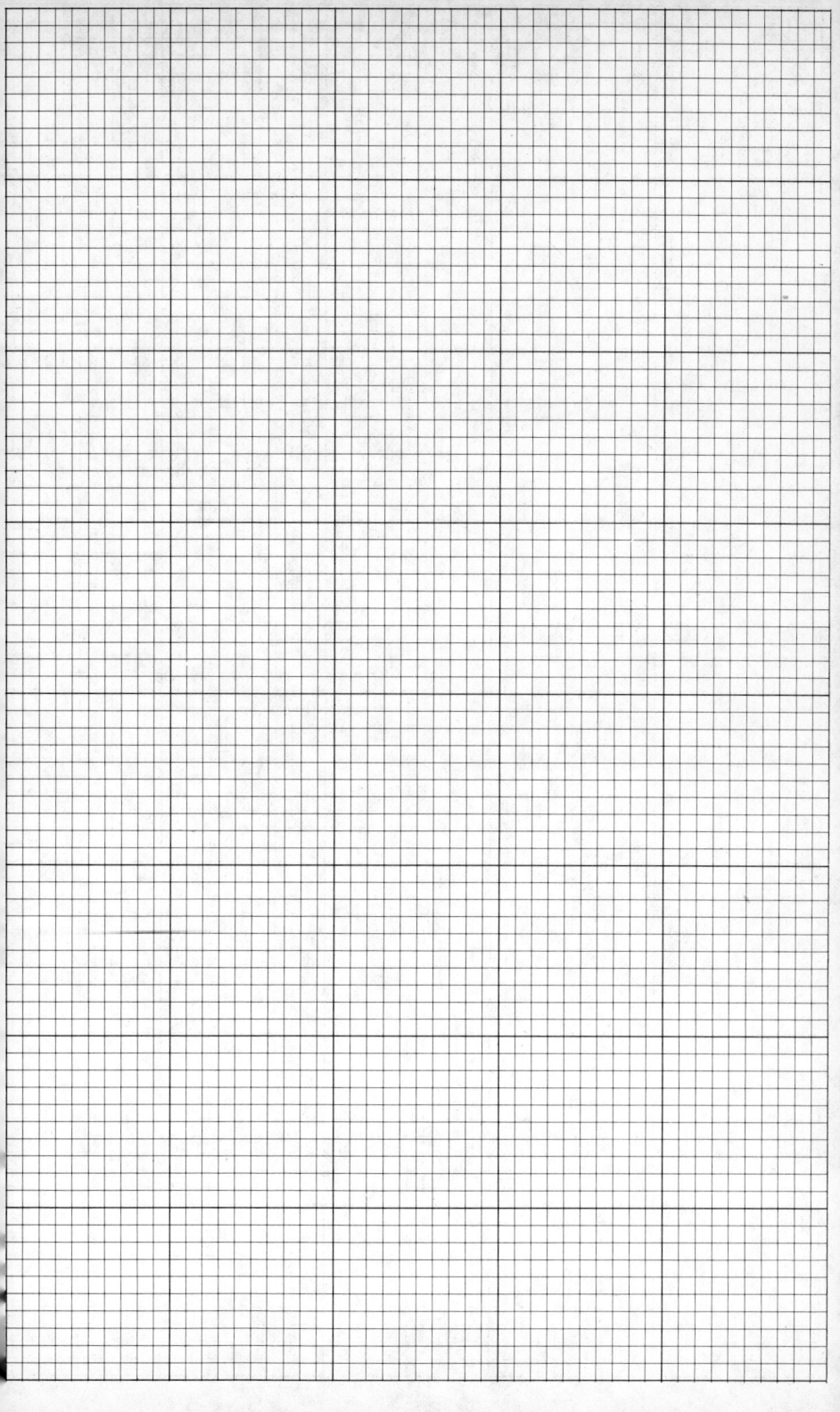

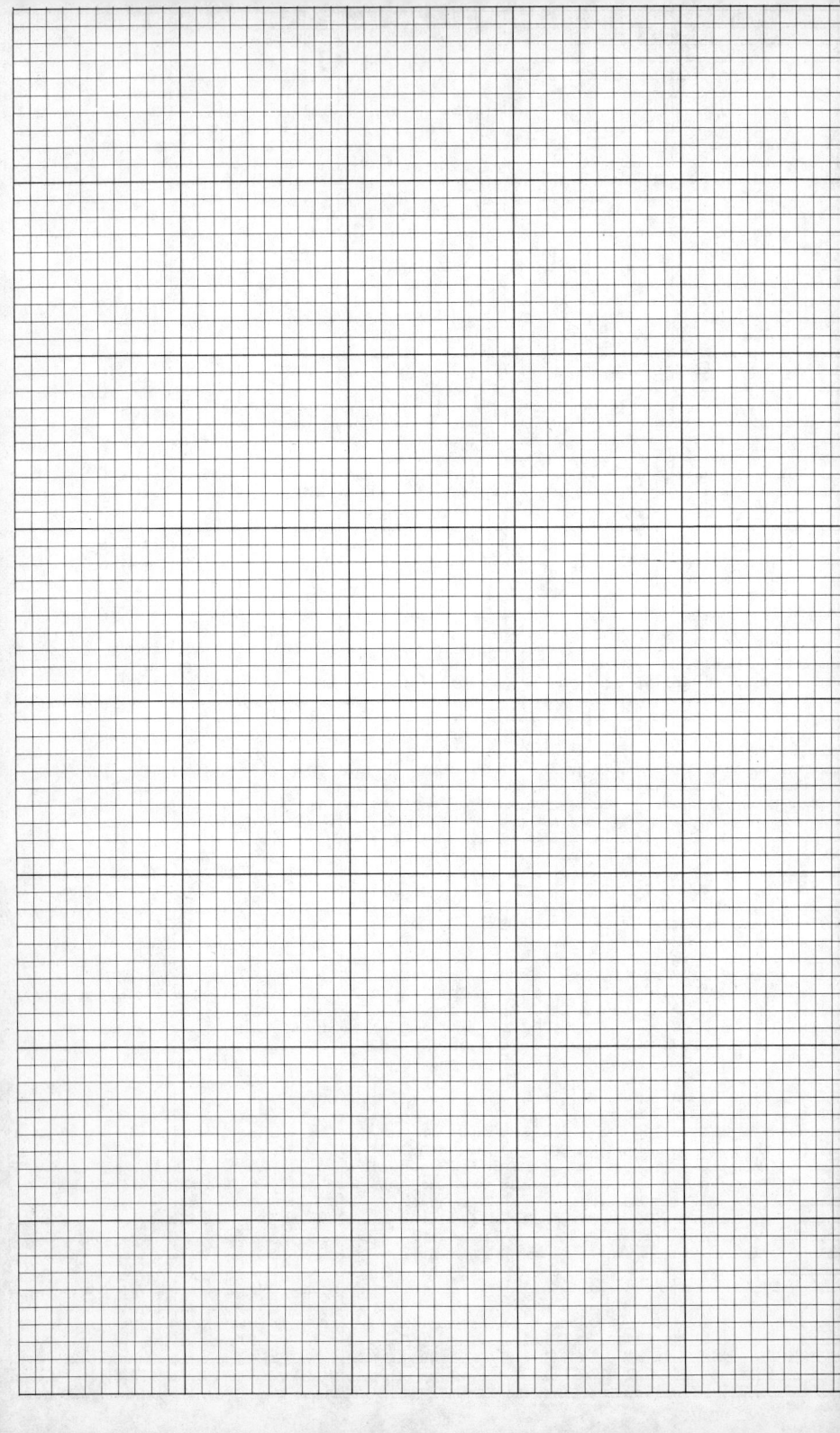

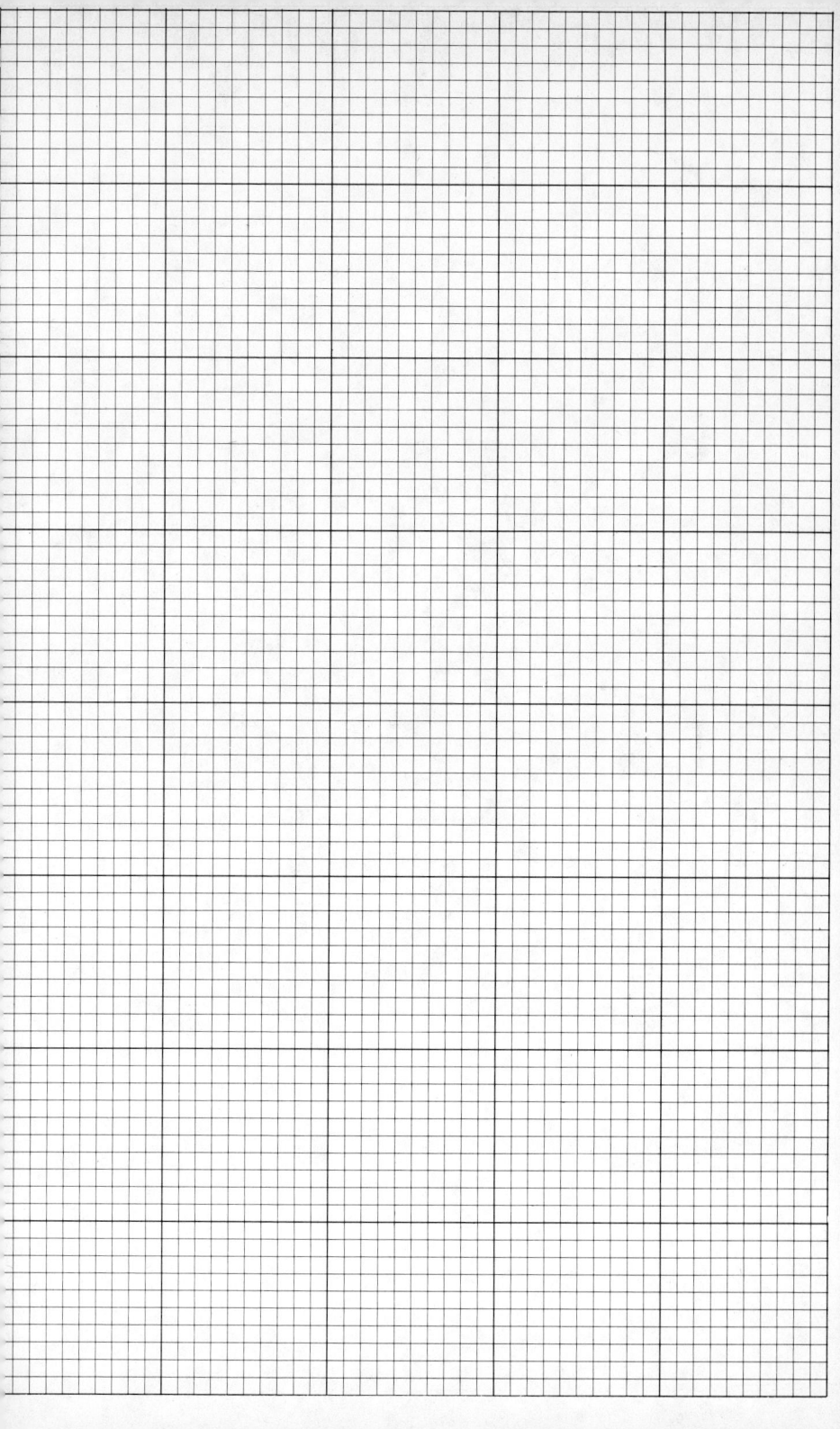

Chapter 3
MEASURES OF CENTRAL TENDENCY

The frequency distribution, along with the histogram and the frequency polygon, is a valuable device which enables us to extract considerable meaning from a mass of data. However, we would like more efficient ways of expressing our results than just a picture of the distribution as a whole. Specifically, we would like to have a statistical method that would yield a *single* value which would tell us something about the entire distribution.

Such a single value is called a *measure of central tendency*. For example, the average income in a community might be $9,000, or the average weight of the defensive line of the Minnesota Vikings might be 245 pounds, or the average test score in a tests-and-measurements course might be 73.2. All of these single values have one thing in common: they are values that best characterize the group as a whole. No person actually had a score of 73.2 on the tests-and-measurements examination, but the average of 73.2 is the best single value that represents the performance of that group of students.

There are a number of measures of central tendency that are designed to give representative values of some distribution. In this chapter we will concentrate on three of the most popular: the arithmetic mean, the median, and the mode.

MEAN

The *average* is a familiar term to all of us, and we remember from arithmetic class that to get the average all we do is add up the numbers and divide by how many numbers there are. This average is called the *arithmetic mean,* or, more commonly, the *mean.* Consider Table 5, where the simple computation of the mean is shown.

Notice that the symbol X refers to a score. The symbol Σ (the Greek letter sigma) means "summation of" or "sum of." Thus, ΣX means "the sum of all the X's," or in other words, "the sum of the scores." N, of course, is the number of cases. By adding the scores, you obtain a value for ΣX. In this example, the sum is 50 and N is 10. So the mean[1] is 5:

$$M = \frac{\Sigma X}{N} = \frac{50}{10} = 5$$

---

[1] The symbol M will be used for the mean throughout this text, but you may also find $\bar{X}$ and occasionally other symbols for the mean in some textbooks.

Table 5

CALCULATION OF THE MEAN

Individual	X
A	2
B	7
C	8
D	6
E	3
F	6
G	2
H	3
I	8
J	5
N = 10	ΣX = 50

$$M = \frac{\Sigma X}{N} = \frac{50}{10}$$

$$M = 5$$

This formula for the mean is for scores which have not been grouped into a frequency distribution. Since most of us work with a relatively small number of scores and have access to one of the popular pocket calculators, this formula for *ungrouped* data will probably be more appropriate. The computational techniques for the mean of *grouped* data, as well as for the other measures of central tendency, are given in the last part of this chapter for those who will need to use grouped data techniques. This will be true of the chapters to follow also: the computational methods for *ungrouped* data will be presented first in each chapter, while *grouped* data techniques will be found towards the end of each chapter.

What is the mean? What does our M = 5 in the example in Table 5 tell us about our data? The mean is the typical performance on a test or task by the group as a whole. When we speak of the average score on an exam, we mean the representative value for this group. The M = 5 in Table 5 states that the value of 5 is the best single value that represents the performance of this group as a whole.

Another useful feature of the mean is that it makes it possible to compare an individual's score with the scores of the rest of the group. Did he score above the mean or below it? Is he above average or below average? How far above or below is he? We can answer these questions in terms of his deviation or distance from the mean.

Instead of reporting an individual's raw score as in Table 5, we could also report his score in terms of its deviation from the mean. For example, individual A's deviation score would be -3, since his raw score is 2 and the mean is 5. Similarly, B's score would be +2, since his raw score is 7 and the mean again is 5. Deviation scores tell us how far each individual's score is from the mean and in which direction. (A positive deviation score shows that the raw score was above the mean, while a negative deviation indicates a score below the mean.)

As was explained previously, the score of any particular individual is denoted by X. An individual's deviation score is denoted by x. Therefore, as a general formula, we can write $x = X - M$. This formula simply states what we noted in a previous paragraph. An individual's deviation score (x) is obtained by subtracting the mean (M) from his raw score (X). Raw scores refer to the scores that we obtained directly from the test.

For Individual A

$x = X - M$

$x = 2 - 5$

$x = -3$

For Individual B

$x = X - M$

$x = 7 - 5$

$x = 2$

Let us repeat Table 5 and express each score as a deviation from the mean. The results are shown in Table 6. Notice that the sum of all of the deviations from the mean (Σx) is zero. This is one of the characteristics of the arithmetic average. It is calculated in such a way that it is directly in the center of these deviations, making the algebraic sum of these deviations zero.

Since the mean takes into account the distances between observations, the measurements from which the mean is calculated must be at least of the interval type. A mean calculated from ordinal data (e.g., a mean rank) may be misleading.

Table 6

RAW SCORES EXPRESSED AS DEVIATION SCORES

Individual	X	x
A	2	-3
B	7	2
C	8	3
D	6	1
E	3	-2
F	6	1
G	2	-3
H	3	-2
I	8	3
J	5	0
N = 10	$\Sigma X = 50$	$\Sigma x = 0$

MODE

The French expression *à la mode* literally means "the vogue," or "in style." That is exactly what the mode is. It is the score that is made the most frequently, or seems to be "in style." The mode is also classified as a measure of central tendency since a glance at a graph of the frequency distribution (see Figure 1 or 2) shows the grouping about a central point, and the mode is the highest point in the hump, or the most frequent score. The mode is easily obtained by inspection, but it is the crudest measure of central tendency. The mode is not as valuable in the analysis of test scores as either the mean or the median. Consider Table 7.

Table 7

CALCULATION OF THE MODE

X	
24	
23	
22	
21	Principal Mode = 21
21	
21	
21	Secondary Mode = 19
20	
19	
19	
19	
18	
17	
16	

The mode here is 21 since four individuals made that score. However, three individuals scored 19, and it is necessary to distinguish between the principal mode and the secondary mode. Whenever there are two peaks or concentrations in a frequency distribution, we have what is known as a *bimodal distribution*. For example, if we were to measure the heights of a random sample of high-school seniors, we would very likely get a bimodal distribution—one peak corresponding to the concentration about an average for girls and another peak for boys.

The chief value of the mode lies in the fact that it is easily obtained by inspection and is useful in locating points of concentration of like scores in a distribution. The mode may be calculated from measurements that are of the ordinal type or above.

MEDIAN

Road signs across the land on our divided highways caution us to "Keep off the median." The median, of course, is the strip of land that divides the lanes that are moving traffic in opposite directions. The median as a measure of central tendency is the point that exactly separates the upper half of the distribution from the lower half. We will see in the next chapter that the median is also the 50th percentile. This follows logically enough, since if the median is at the exact center of a distribution, 50% of the scores would fall below the median.

The median can be computed easily for *ungrouped data* if a set of scores is arranged in order of magnitude, with the highest score at the top, and the lowest score at the bottom. It can then be computed by counting up from the *bottom* $\frac{N+1}{2}$ scores.

In Table 8, N (the number of scores) is an odd number, 9. $\frac{N+1}{2} = \frac{9+1}{2} = 5$. We then count up from the bottom 5 scores, and find that the fifth score is 14, and this is the median for this distribution.

Table 8

CALCULATION OF THE MEDIAN, N IS ODD

X
16
15
15
14
14
13
12
10
9
N = 9

Med = $\frac{N+1}{2} = \frac{9+1}{2}$ = 5th score from the bottom

5th score is 14

If N is an even number, such as in Table 9, we calculate $\frac{N+1}{2} = \frac{10+1}{2} = 5.5$ scores from the bottom. Counting up from the bottom, the fifth score is 10, and the sixth score is 12. The median is halfway between 10 and 12, so the value of the median for this distribution would be 11.

Table 9

CALCULATION OF THE MEDIAN, N IS EVEN

X
15
14
14
13
12
10
9
8
6
3
N = 10

$$\text{Med} = \frac{N+1}{2} = \frac{10+1}{2} = 5.5\text{th score from the bottom}$$

$$\text{Med} = 11$$

As with the mean, the median does not have to be an actual score made by an individual. The median satisfies the definition as being the central point in the distribution, and with an even number of scores (as in Table 9) this value may not exist in the distribution. However, it is a measure of central tendency in that it shows the central point in the distribution.

The median can be helpful in working with test grades, since it is easily computed from a simple frequency distribution that you should make after scoring a set of test papers. In Table 4 in the last chapter was a simple frequency distribution of 50 English exam scores. Counting up from the bottom the required 25.5 scores, you find that the 25th and 26th scores are both 81. So, the median for this set of scores is 81.

The median is also valuable in that it is an accurate measure of central tendency for measurements that are only of the ordinal type. Since no assumptions are made concerning distances between observation points, it is meaningful to talk about median ranks, for example. So the median is an appropriate measure of central tendency for data that are ordinal or above.

COMPARING THE MEAN, MEDIAN AND MODE

If a measure of central tendency is a single value that best represents the performance of the group as a whole, which single value should be used? If you compute the mean, median, and mode for the same set of scores, you very rarely will find that all three are identical. The question we then ask regards which one is the best measure to use—which one will give us the "best single value" that describes the entire distribution?

The answer to this question is by no means a simple one. First of all, we can ignore the mode since it is a pretty crude measure of central tendency. This leaves the mean and median to be considered, and as you probably have guessed, the mean is most often given as a measure of central tendency. Whenever you see the term "average" used in books, magazines and newspapers in describing some distribution, most often the mean is what is being referred to.

However, there are many instances where the median is a valuable statistic. Since it is not affected by extreme or atypical values as much as is the mean, it is useful in situations where the distribution is either positively or negatively skewed. For example, suppose we would like to calculate the average income for people living in a small midwestern town. Let us further assume that in this community there is one millionaire and the rest of the residents are earning what we would judge to be ordinary incomes. This is a slight exaggeration, but it will serve to illustrate the usefulness of the median when distributions are markedly skewed. The mean, since it takes into account the exact value of each score, would be unduly influenced by the millionaire's income, and the measure of central tendency would be much too high. The median, on the other hand, is the center of the distribution and would not be affected very much by the addition of a single score at the extreme end. Clearly, the median would give the most accurate picture of the income for this situation.

This can be demonstrated very easily by the data of Table 9. The median is 11 and the mean is 104/10 = 10.4. Let us add a score of 100 to this distribution. The median now would be 12 and the mean would be 204/11 = 18.5. It should be obvious that the addition of a single extreme score affects the median only slightly, but can cause quite a change in the mean.

As a further illustration of this point, let us examine the data of Table 10 and compute the three measures of central tendency for this distribution.

<u>Mode</u>: the most frequent score is 10

<u>Median</u>: $\frac{N+1}{2} = \frac{18+1}{2} = 9.5$ scores from the bottom is 9

<u>Mean</u>: $M = \frac{\Sigma X}{N} = \frac{156}{18} = 8.7$

It is obvious in this example that the slight difference in the three measures of central tendency is caused by several low scores that tend to "pull" the value of the mean towards the low end of the distribution. If you would refer to Figures 4 and 5 in the previous chapter we can make a generalization concerning skewness and measures of central tendency.

In Figure 4 there is negative skewness with a few extreme low scores; therefore, the mean would be pulled to the left of the median, so the value of the mean would be smaller. *If the mean is significantly smaller than the median, the distribution is negatively skewed.*

Table 10

COMPARISON OF THE THREE MEASURES
OF CENTRAL TENDENCY

	$\overline{X}$
	15
	14
	14
	12
	11
	10
	10
	10
	9
	9
	8
	7
	6
	6
	5
	4
	4
	2
$\Sigma X =$	$\overline{156}$
$N =$	18

In Figure 5 there is positive skewness with a few extreme high scores; therefore, the mean would be pulled to the right of the median, and the value of the mean would be larger. *If the mean is significantly larger than the median, the distribution is positively skewed.*

GROUPED DATA TECHNIQUES

There are times when it is convenient to be able to calculate measures of central tendency for data that are in the form of a grouped frequency distribution. The computational techniques for grouped data are valuable as a shortcut method if a calculator is not available, and they may be an absolute necessity for determining measures of central tendency when you have only the grouped frequency distribution from a newspaper article or some other summary report. Frequency distributions were described in detail in the last chapter, so it might be a good idea to review that material thoroughly before beginning this section.

It is necessary to define some terms to be used in these computational techniques. All have been referred to in the previous chapter, but not in a precise manner. Table 3 from the last chapter is reprinted below so you can easily compare the new terminology with your previous acquaintance with Table 3.

Table 3

A BETTER ILLUSTRATION OF THE GROUPED FREQUENCY DISTRIBUTION FOR THE ENGLISH ACHIEVEMENT SCORES

Scores	Frequency
95-99	2
90-94	6
85-89	8
80-84	12
75-79	7
70-74	7
65-69	5
60-64	3
	N = 50

N is the number of observations in the frequency distribution. The value of N in Table 3 is 50.

f is the number of observations in each interval (the frequency). The value of f for the top interval (95-99) in Table 3 is 2. As noted earlier, the sum of the f values for all the intervals must equal N.

i is the size of the interval. In Table 3 the value of i is 5, since each interval could contain five different values. For example, the interval 80-84 could contain scores of 80, 81, 82, 83, or 84; thus, i = 5, since five different values are represented.

L is the exact lower limit of any interval. The top interval in Table 3 is 95-99, and the next interval is 90-94. For purposes of calculations, we must precisely state a lower limit. The value of L in the top interval is 94.5, and for the next interval, 89.5. In other words, L is always one-half step below the limits of the bottom number in any interval. In the interval 65-69, for example, the value of L would be 64.5.

Mp is the midpoint of any interval. This value is exactly midway between the upper and lower numbers of any interval. For example, in Table 3 the top interval has a midpoint of 97, since this value is exactly midway between 95 and 99. To calculate Mp it is only necessary to average the upper and lower numbers of the interval. Sometimes Mp might be a fraction instead of a whole number. For example, if the interval were 70-79, the Mp would be $(70 + 79)/2 = 149/2 = 74.5$.

Mean

Table 11 shows 50 scores on a biology lab exam, and the computation of the mean from grouped data follows the table. Note that Table 11 is an ordinary frequency distribution but that two more columns, d and fd, have been added.

Table 11

CALCULATION OF THE MEAN FOR BIOLOGY SCORES, GROUPED DATA

Scores	f	d	fd
85-89	1	3	3
80-84	3	2	6
75-79	6	1	6
70-74	15	0	
65-69	12	-1	-12
60-64	8	-2	-16
55-59	3	-3	- 9
50-54	2	-4	- 8
	N = 50		Σfd = -30

(+15 for the upper positive values; -45 for the lower negative values)

To obtain the entries in the d column, one of the intervals is chosen as the "origin" and a zero is placed in the d column opposite that interval. *Any* interval can be chosen, but it is usually preferable to choose one in the center of the distribution because this results in smaller numbers for your calculations. In Table 11 we have picked the 70-74 interval as the origin and placed a zero in the d column.

The next step is to count up by units (+1, +2, etc.) from the zero until you reach the top of the distribution. Then count down (-1, -2, etc.) from the zero until you reach the bottom of the distribution. The value of d, then, is simply the distance each interval is from the one chosen as the origin. For example, the 55-59 interval is 3 intervals below the 70-74 interval.

To obtain the entries in the fd column, simply multiply f by d for each interval. Thus, in Table 11, 1 × 3 = 3, 3 × 2 = 6, and so on. Do the same for all the intervals, remembering that some of the fd values will be negative since some of the d values are negative.

The next step is to obtain the algebraic sum of the fd column by adding the positive values (15) and the negative values (-45). This quantity is known as Σfd, and in Table 11, Σfd = -30.

The formula for the mean using the data in Table 11 is:

$$M = M_p + i\left(\frac{\Sigma fd}{N}\right), \text{ where}$$

M_p is the midpoint of the interval at the origin, 72
i is the size of the interval, 5
N is the number of scores, 50
Σfd is the sum of the fd column, -30

Substituting in the formula, we get:

$$M = 72 + 5\left(\frac{-30}{50}\right)$$

$$= 72 + \left(\frac{-150}{50}\right)$$

$$= 72 + (-3)$$

$$M = 69$$

The mean for the distribution of biology lab exam scores of Table 11 is 69. As a check on the accuracy of your calculations, use a different interval as the origin for the d column. For example, if you choose 55-59 as the origin, $M_p = 57$, $i = 5$, $N = 50$, and $\Sigma fd = 120$. If you substitute these new values in the formula, you will find the mean is still 69. No matter where the zero is placed in the d column, the mean will always be the same.

Median

Since the median is the 50th percentile, we want to find the point in a frequency distribution that separates the top half of the scores from the bottom

Table 12

CALCULATION OF THE MEDIAN FOR GEOGRAPHY QUIZ SCORES, GROUPED DATA

Scores	f	Calculations
75-79	2	(a) 50% of 54 = 27
70-74	4	
65-69	8	(b) 2 + 3 + 6 + 15 = 26
60-64	14	
55-59	15	(c) R = 27 - 26 = 1
50-54	6	
45-49	3	(d) $F_{50} = 14$
40-44	2	
N = 54		(e) L = 59.5

half. Table 12 shows the calculation of the 50th percentile, P_{50}, for a distribution of scores on a geography quiz.

The first step in the calculation of the median or P_{50} is to take 50% of N. In step (a), $.50 \times 54 = 27$.

The next step is to count up from the bottom of the f column by adding each frequency until we get as close to 27 as we can, without exceeding 27. In step (b) we see that $2 + 3 + 6 + 15 = 26$. If we went up one more f value, we would go beyond 27, so we must stop here. This tells us that the median or P_{50} is in the *next* interval—somewhere between 59.5 and 64.5.

The next step is to subtract the frequencies that we have just totaled from the value that we actually needed. We needed 50% of N or 27, but could total only 26. So in step (c), $27 - 26 = 1$. This remainder is called R.

Next we inspect the interval that contains the median and find out the frequency for this interval. Looking at Table 12 we note that there are 14 scores in the 60-64 interval. We call this value F_{50}, the frequency of the interval containing the 50th percentile. Thus, in step (d), $F_{50} = 14$.

Finally, we determine the exact lower limit, L, for the interval containing the median. Since this interval is 60-64, $L = 59.5$.

We are now ready to substitute in the formula below.

$$\text{Median} = L + i \left(\frac{R}{F_{50}}\right), \text{ where}$$

L is the exact lower limit of the interval containing the median
i is the size of the interval
R is the remainder after subtracting necessary frequencies from 50% of N
F_{50} is the frequency of the interval containing the median

From our example in Table 12,

$$\text{Median} = 59.5 + 5\left(\frac{1}{14}\right)$$

$$= 59.5 + \frac{5}{14}$$

$$= 59.5 + .4$$

$$\text{Median} = 59.9$$

So the median or P_{50} is 59.9, and we say that 50% of the distribution falls below 59.9.

Mode

As we noted earlier the mode is the score that appears most frequently in a distribution of scores. Since the actual identity of each individual score is lost when the scores are grouped in a frequency distribution, we can only make an assumption concerning the value of the mode when we use grouped data.

This value is called the *crude mode,* and it is simply the midpoint of the interval with the greatest frequency. In other words, we find the interval that contains the greatest number of scores and assume that the midpoint of the interval was the score made most often. You can see why this value is called the *crude mode!*

If you refer to Table 11, you will note that the interval containing the greatest number of scores is 70-74, so the crude mode would be 72. And in Table 12, the crude mode would be the midpoint of the 55-59 interval, or 57.

Concluding Remarks on Grouped Data

The statistics computed by the grouped data techniques presented here, as well as those to follow in subsequent chapters, will usually be slightly different from those computed directly from the raw data itself. This is due to the fact that certain assumptions are involved in the derivation of the grouped data formulas. However, when the N is over 30 or so, the differences are usually quite small, and the results from the grouped data can be considered quite accurate.

PROBLEMS

1. The following data consist of 20 scores on a spelling test.

X	x
21	
20	
20	
17	
17	
16	
16	
16	
16	
15	
15	
12	
12	
10	
9	
8	
8	
7	
3	
2	
$\Sigma X=$	$\Sigma x=$

a. Calculate the mean.

$M =$

b. Check your answer by subtracting the mean from each score. If your mean is correct, the algebraic sum of the deviations from the mean should equal zero.

2. The following 20 scores were obtained on a psychology quiz.

X
31
31
30
30
28
28
28
28
26
25
24
23
23
22
16
15
15
14
12
11

a. Calculate the mean, the median, and the mode.

Mean =

Median =

Mode =

b. Which of the three is the poorest measure of central tendency for this data?

3. The following data show 15 scores on a short vocabulary test.

X
31
27
25
25
20
20
17
17
17
14
14
11
11
10
8

Calculate the mean, the median, and the mode.

Mean =

Median =

Mode =

4. The following frequency distribution shows the scores made by 60 pupils on a physical fitness test.

Scores	f	d	fd
60-62	2		
57-59	6		
54-56	9		
51-53	12		
48-50	16		
45-47	8		
42-44	6		
39-41	1		
	N = 60		

Using the formulas for grouped data, calculate the mean, the median, and the mode.

Mean =

Median =

Mode =

5. Seventy students in accelerated classes in ninth-grade mathematics are given a standardized mathematics examination, with the following results:

Scores	f	d	fd
70-79	3		
60-69	11		
50-59	16		
40-49	14		
30-39	10		
20-29	9		
10-19	4		
0-9	3		
	N = 70		

a. Calculate the mean, the median, and the mode.

Mean =

Median =

Mode =

b. Graph this frequency distribution on a sheet of graph paper, using either a histogram or frequency polygon. Label the mean, median, and mode on the x-axis, using the values you calculated in part a.

c. What kind of skewness is present in this situation?

d. What is the cause of this skewness?

Chapter 4

PERCENTILES AND NORMS

If little Johnny Smith comes home to report to his mother that he got a score of 35 on a nationwide achievement test in arithmetic, how should his mother react? She would certainly want a little more information before she decides either to give him a quarter for some candy or take away his TV privileges for the evening. What was the total number of possible points that he could score? A score of 35 on a 100-point test is considerably different than the same score on a 40-point test. Another question that Johnny's mother might want answered concerns where Johnny is in relation to the rest of his class or to the group of children at his age or at his grade in the entire nation.

Clearly the simple raw score does not give us very much information. In fact, it could even be misleading. Johnny's mother would not be the first to believe that a score of 35 means that he got 35% of the questions correct. So, what we need to have is some uniform method by which we can tell where Johnny stands in relation to the rest of his group. One such method involves the use of *norms,* which have been constructed on the basis of some comparison group. Test publishers try out their tests on a relatively small representative sample, and the results of this sample make up the norms that we use for making our comparisons. More will be said about the process of test construction in Chapter 7.

There are several kinds of norms used for making comparisons, and we will consider two of the most widely used—age-grade norms and percentile norms.

AGE-GRADE NORMS

After the test publisher has administered the test to what he considers representative samples of students of various ages and in various grades, norms are constructed that list the raw score, the equivalent age, and equivalent grade corresponding to that raw score. As an example, let us say that this test publisher has constructed a test in arithmetic achievement and, after appropriate sampling, comes up with the norms shown in Table 13.

It becomes immediately apparent that a raw score takes on a lot more meaning when interpreted in terms of age-grade norms. Johnny's score of 35 means that his test performance was comparable with that of the "average" 10-year-old or the "average" fourth-grader during the seventh month of the fourth grade. All that is left to know to interpret Johnny's raw score is his age and his grade. If he has just turned 9 years old, we would say that he is definitely above average in his grasp of arithmetic.

Table 13

AGE-GRADE EQUIVALENTS ON AN ARITHMETIC ACHIEVEMENT TEST

Raw Score	Grade	Age	Raw Score	Grade	Age
50	8.0	13-4	30	4.0	9-4
49	7.6	13-0	29	4.0	9-3
48	7.3	12-9	28	3.8	9-2
47	7.1	12-6	27	3.8	9-0
46	6.8	12-2	26	3.6	8-11
45	6.5	11-11	25	3.5	8-10
44	6.2	11-7	24	3.5	8-8
43	6.0	11-5	23	3.3	8-7
42	5.8	11-2	22	3.3	8-6
41	5.6	10-11	21	3.1	8-5
40	5.4	10-8	20	3.0	8-4
39	5.2	10-6	19	3.0	8-3
38	5.0	10-4	18	2.8	8-2
37	4.9	10-3	17	2.8	8-1
36	4.7	10-1	16	2.7	8-0
35	4.7	10-0	15	2.5	7-11
34	4.5	9-10	14	2.3	7-9
33	4.3	9-9	13	2.2	7-8
32	4.3	9-7	12	2.1	7-7
31	4.1	9-6	11	2.0	7-6

As with virtually all statistics, caution must be exercised in the interpretation of age-grade norms. It would be tempting to say that since Johnny is performing as well as the average 10-year-old, he would have the same knowledge of arithmetic fundamentals that the average 10-year-old has. This is *not* true and is the reason why quotation marks appeared around "average" in the preceding paragraph. Johnny's superior score, which was equal to that of the average 10-year-old, is very likely due to his superior mastery of the material at his own level.

He picks up more points at this level than the average student who is a year older but does not do as well on more advanced material that is completely foreign to him. In spite of this shortcoming, age-grade norms are valuable in comparing the progress of children in a classroom setting.

PERCENTILE NORMS

Probably even more familiar and more widely used are percentile norms. The test publisher administers the test to a large number of examinees to obtain norms, and an individual score is located in regard to the percentage of the distribution falling below it. Many tests have several sets of norms, depending on the purpose of the test. For example, a test of mechanical skills might have norms based on a group of diesel mechanics at a trade school, or a group of high-school senior home economics students, or a class of college sophomores in a predentistry curriculum. More will be said later in Chapter 7 on the importance of choosing the correct set of norms.

The percentile is a way of expressing the location of a particular raw score in a distribution. In the last chapter we found that the median is that point in a distribution below which lie 50% of the scores. In exactly the same way we could calculate points below which lie 20%, 43%, 68%, or any percentage of the scores. These points are called *percentiles* and are usually denoted by the symbol P_p, where P is a percentile and p is the percentage of the cases below that point. P_{20} (read "a percentile of 20" or "the 20th percentile"), for example, is the point below which lie 20% of the scores. Similarly, P_{68} would be the point below which lie 68% of the scores. Obviously, the median would be P_{50}.

To use percentile norms, all we have to do is locate a student's raw score in a table of norms and find what percentage of the distribution (the standardization group) falls below. For example, if the student received a raw score of 105 on a particular standardized test, and this is equivalent to the 82nd percentile, this would mean that 82% of the standardization group scored below him.

A set of norms for a college entrance exam is reprinted in Table 14. Note how easy it is to interpret any given raw score in terms of the standardization group. For example, a raw score of 23 is at the 64th percentile; that is, 64% of the original group scored lower than 23.

You will often run across the term *percentile rank* (PR) in a discussion of percentiles. To avoid confusion, just remember that if you want to know the score below which a *given percentage* of the distribution falls, you are talking about a percentile. Thus, the 45th percentile in Table 14 is a score of 21. However, if you are interested in knowing what percentage falls below a *given score,* you are dealing with the score's *percentile rank*. Therefore, in Table 14, the percentile rank of a score of 21 is 45.

Another feature of percentiles is that they can be used to compare an individual's own performance on two or more tests. This is valuable since it is impossible to compare raw scores directly. Knowing that an individual scored 27 on a

Table 14

PERCENTILES ON A COLLEGE ENTRANCE EXAMINATION

Raw Score	Percentile
31	99
30	98
29	97
28	94
27	90
26	86
25	79
24	72
23	64
22	55
21	45
20	36
19	29
18	23
17	17
16	12
15	7
14	5
13	4
12	2
5-11	1

reading test, 54 on an arithmetic achievement test, and 128 on a mechanical aptitude test does not help us know his relative strengths or weaknesses. However, if we know that his three scores were at the 76th, 53rd, and 83rd percentiles, respectively, we know quite a bit about his performance in relation to the rest of the examinees.

CALCULATION OF PERCENTILES FROM GROUPED DATA

It is sometimes convenient to be able to calculate a given percentile from scores that have been grouped into a frequency distribution. Percentiles can be calculated for measurements that are of the ordinal type or above. The computational steps for calculating percentiles are shown in Table 15. In this example we would like to know what score corresponds to the 65th percentile. (Note that the technique for calculating percentiles is almost identical with the method described in Chapter 3 for calculating the median.)

The first step is to calculate the percentage of N shown by the percentile. In step (a), 65% of 50 is 32.5.

The next step is to count up from the bottom of the f column by adding each frequency until we get as close to 32.5 as we can, without exceeding 32.5. In (b) we see that 2 + 3 + 8 + 12 = 25. If we went up one more f value, we would go beyond 32.5, so we must stop here. This tells us that the score corresponding to P_{65} is in the *next* interval—somewhere between 69.5 and 74.5.

The next step is to subtract the frequencies that we have totaled, from the value which we actually needed. Thus in (c), 32.5 - 25 = 7.5. This remainder is called R.

Table 15

CALCULATION OF PERCENTILES, GROUPED DATA

Scores	f	Calculations
85-89	1	(a) 65% of 50 = 32.5
80-84	3	(b) 2 + 3 + 8 + 12 = 25
75-79	6	(c) R = 32.5 - 25 = 7.5
70-74	15	(d) Fp = 15
65-69	12	(e) L = 69.5
60-64	8	
55-59	3	
50-54	2	
N =	50	

Next we inspect the interval that contains P_{65}, and find out the frequency contained in this interval. In Table 15 there are 15 scores in the interval 70-74, so we call this value Fp, the frequency of the interval containing the given percentile. Thus in (d) Fp = 15.

Finally, we determine the exact lower limit, L, for the interval containing P_{65}. Since this interval is 70-74, obviously L = 69.5.

We are now ready to substitute in the formula below.

$$P_p = L + i \left(\frac{R}{F_p}\right), \text{where}$$

    L is the exact lower limit of class containing P_p
    i is the size of the interval
    R is the remainder after subtracting necessary frequencies from the given percent of N
    Fp is the frequency of the interval containing P_p

For our example in Table 15,

$$P_{65} = 69.5 + 5 \left(\frac{7.5}{15}\right)$$

Percentiles and Norms

$$= 69.5 + \left(\frac{37.5}{15}\right)$$

$$= 69.5 + 2.5$$

$$P_{65} = 72$$

As we see from this example, $P_{65} = 72$. In other words 65% of the scores fell below a score of 72.

PROBLEMS

1. John has just finished the third grade and scores 19 on the arithmetic achievement test whose norms are shown in Table 13. What can you say about his performance?

2. Karen scores 27 on the same arithmetic test. If she is 7 years and 11 months old, why is it incorrect to say that she has the same proficiency as the average 9-year-old?

3. What entrance exam score corresponds to the 36th percentile on the norms shown in Table 14? What is the percentile rank of a score of 24?

4. Calculate P_{30}, P_{64}, and P_{90} for the following set of scores.

Scores	f
70-79	2
60-69	7
50-59	14
40-49	25
30-39	13
20-29	7
10-19	9
0-9	3
	N = 80

Percentiles and Norms

a. P_{30} =

b. P_{64} =

c. P_{90} =

5. From the distribution shown in Table 15, calculate P_{50}, P_{90}, and P_{22}.

   a. $P_{50} =$

   b. $P_{90} =$

   c. $P_{22} =$

Chapter 5
MEASURES OF VARIABILITY

MEANING OF VARIABILITY

One characteristic of people and things that is obvious from even a casual observation is their variability. Some people are short, some are tall, others are in-between. One 5-year-old might be forward, aggressive, and noisy, while her playmate is withdrawn, passive, and quiet. A teacher giving a test may find that a few of his seventh-graders get high scores, a few get very low scores, and most scores cluster in the center of the group. You may notice that your car averages 14 miles per gallon, but you know that on a long trip you can coax 17 out of it, while in heavy traffic the mileage drops to a mere 8.

We said earlier that the task of statistics was to reduce large masses of data to some meaningful values. In Chapter 3 you saw how a measure of central tendency yielded the best *single* value that described the performance of the group as a whole. It was a value that best represented the entire group of observations. But as the preceding paragraph indicates, there is more to describing a group of observations than noting the *average* performance, because a measure of central tendency tells you nothing concerning the variation about the average. In preparing frequency distributions and calculating measures of central tendency in earlier chapters, you noted that some scores fell below the mean while others were above it. *The fluctuation of scores about a measure of central tendency is called variability.*

We frequently use measures of variability to compare two sets of test scores. The mean alone is not enough, since the means of the two sets could be identical, yet the distributions could be very dissimilar.

In Table 16, the means of the two groups are identical, but notice how dissimilar the two distributions are. Obviously, we need more than just the mean to know the characteristics of our distribution of scores.

THE RANGE

One of the simplest and most straightforward measures of variation about a mean is the *range*. The range can be calculated for measurements that are of the ordinal type or above. The range, as we mentioned previously, is the distance between the two extreme scores. For example, if the highest score in a distribution is 97 and the lowest is 65, the range is 97 - 65 = 32. This value tells us something about the dispersion of our distribution. (Note that we will be using a number of different words to describe variability—dispersion, variation, scattering, etc.; all of these terms imply variability about the mean.) The larger the

Table 16

TWO DISTRIBUTIONS WITH EQUAL MEANS BUT DIFFERENT RANGES

Distribution I		Distribution II	
X		X	
10		12	
9		12	
8	$M_1 = 7$	12	$M_2 = 7$
8		11	
7		10	
7		5	
6		4	
6		2	
5		1	
4		1	
$\Sigma X_1 = 70$		$\Sigma X_2 = 70$	
N = 10		N = 10	

range, the larger is the dispersion of scores from the mean value. In Table 16, the means are identical but the range for Distribution I is 10 - 4 = 6, and for Distribution II it is 12 - 1 = 11. Obviously, the scores in Distribution II are scattered more widely about the mean than are the scores in Distribution I.

Although the range is a good preliminary measure of variability, it suffers from two drawbacks. One problem is that a single extreme value can greatly alter the range. In Distribution II of Table 16, a score of 17 would increase the range from 7 to 16. Another problem is that the range is based on only two scores (the highest and the lowest) and does not tell us anything about the pattern of the variability. Consider Table 17.

In both distributions in Table 17, the ranges are equal (7) and means are almost equal (14.2 and 14.0). But look how different the two distributions are. Distribution I has a high score of 17 and a low of 10. Notice that the rest of the values are tightly grouped around the center of the distribution. Distribution II has the same extreme values, 17 and 10, but notice that the rest of the values are tightly grouped towards the ends of the distribution with a gap in the middle. It is evident that the range does not tell us all we need to know about the variability of a set of scores. We need to have a measure of variability that takes into account the pattern of the distribution. Such a measure is the *standard deviation*.

THE STANDARD DEVIATION

As we mentioned in a previous chapter, each score in a distribution varies from the mean by a greater or lesser amount (except, of course, when the score

Table 17

TWO DISTRIBUTIONS WITH EQUAL RANGES BUT DISSIMILAR PATTERNS OF DISPERSION

Distribution I		Distribution II	
X		X	
17		17	
15		17	
15	$M = \dfrac{142}{10} = 14.2$	17	$M_2 = \dfrac{140}{10} = 14$
15		17	
15		16	
14	$R_1 = 17 - 10 = 7$	16	$R_2 = 17 - 10 = 7$
14		10	
14		10	
13		10	
10		10	
$\Sigma X = 142$		$\Sigma X = 140$	
$N = 10$		$N = 10$	

is the same as the mean value). It would seem obvious, then, that we might measure the amount of variability about the mean by using the deviations of each score from the mean. In Table 6 we did exactly that by finding the deviation value (x) for each score.

A measure of variability could be the average value of these deviations from the mean. However, you saw that the sum of these deviations (Σx) about the mean is always equal to zero. This makes it arithmetically impossible to work with. The problem, then, is to find some way to get rid of the negative signs in front of the deviations. We can get rid of all of the negative numbers by squaring the deviations. You will remember from elementary algebra that when two numbers of the same sign are multiplied together the product is always positive. So when we square each of the deviations, we get positive numbers whether our original deviations are negative or positive. Of course we will eventually have to take a square root in order to get back to the original units of measurement. The sum of the squared deviations is divided by N, and the square root of this quantity is called the standard deviation. The standard deviation can be calculated from any set of measurements that are at least of the interval type. The formula that represents the standard deviation is:

$$SD = \sqrt{\dfrac{\Sigma x^2}{N}}, \text{ where}$$

  SD is the standard deviation
  Σx^2 refers to the sum of all squared deviations from the mean
  N is the number of scores

Measures of Variability

Table 18

CALCULATION OF STANDARD DEVIATION
(DEVIATION METHOD)

X	x	x^2	
15	5	25	
14	4	16	
12	2	4	$SD = \sqrt{\dfrac{\Sigma x^2}{N}} = \sqrt{\dfrac{128}{10}}$
12	2	4	
11	1	1	
10	0	0	
9	-1	1	$= \sqrt{12.8}$
8	-2	4	
7	-3	9	
2	-8	64	SD = 3.58
$\Sigma X = 100$	0	$\Sigma x^2 = 128$	
N = 10			

Table 18 shows the computation of the standard deviation using this formula.

The above example shows the calculation of SD by use of the deviation method. However, it is laborious to compute since it is necessary to compute the mean, subtract the mean from each score, square these deviations, average these deviations, and extract the square root. A simpler formula has been developed which will give the same results with much less work. The formula is:

$$SD = \sqrt{\frac{\Sigma X^2}{N} - M^2}, \text{ where}$$

ΣX^2 refers to the sum of squared scores
M is the mean
N is the number of scores

This formula is mathematically the same, and it is much easier to compute. The method using this formula is called the whole score method, because the original whole scores are used instead of the deviations. Notice that in the above formula it is ΣX^2, which is the sum of the squares of the whole scores, whereas in a previous formula it was Σx^2, the squares of the deviations. Table 19 shows the calculation of the SD using the whole score formula.

Just what does an SD value tell us about the nature of the distribution? Obviously, it tells us *how much* the scores in a distribution deviate from the mean. If the value of the SD is small, there is little variability, and the majority of the scores are tightly clustered about the mean. If the SD is large, the scores are more widely scattered above and below the mean. We can use the SD for comparing two groups to see how they differ in variability. For example, let us repeat Table 17, in which we illustrated two groups, one with scores tightly

Table 19

CALCULATION OF STANDARD DEVIATION
(WHOLE SCORE METHOD)

X	X^2
12	144
12	144
14	196
17	289
14	196
13	169
16	256
15	225
15	225
15	225
$\Sigma X = 143$	$\Sigma X^2 = 2069$

$N = 10$

$M = \dfrac{143}{10} = 14.3$

$M^2 = (14.3)^2 = 204.5$

Substitute:

$SD = \sqrt{\dfrac{\Sigma X^2}{N} - M^2}$

$= \sqrt{\dfrac{2069}{10} - 204.5}$

$= \sqrt{206.9 - 204.5}$

$= \sqrt{2.4}$

$SD = 1.55$

grouped and another group in which the scores were more widely scattered. These results are shown in Table 20.

Distribution II has an SD almost twice as large as Distribution I. This is due to the different patterns in the distribution. The means are almost equal and the ranges are equal, but the distributions are patterned differently and the SD gives us this information.

The importance of the SD cannot be overemphasized. Because the concept of the SD is basic to the construction and interpretation of tests, the student should familiarize himself with the preceding discussion and calculations.

The steps illustrated in Table 19 are:
1. Place the scores in the column X.
2. Square each score and enter the results in the column X^2.
3. Sum each of the columns to obtain ΣX and ΣX^2.
4. Compute the mean.
5. Square the mean.
6. Substitute in the formula for ΣX^2, N, and M^2.
7. Perform the necessary calculations under the square root sign.
8. Extract the square root.

THE SD AND THE NORMAL CURVE

We noted in Chapter 2 that much of the data in education and in the behavioral sciences are normally distributed; that is, the distribution of scores closely

Table 20

COMPARISON OF THE SD'S FOR TWO DISTRIBUTIONS

Distribution I			Distribution II		
X	X^2		X	X^2	
17	289	$N = 10$	17	289	$N = 10$
15	225	$M = \frac{142}{10} = 14.2$	17	289	$M = \frac{140}{10} = 14$
15	225		17	289	
15	225	$M^2 = 201.6$	17	289	$M^2 = 196$
15	225		16	256	
14	196	$SD = \sqrt{\frac{\Sigma X^2}{N} - M^2}$	16	256	$SD = \sqrt{\frac{\Sigma X^2}{N} - M^2}$
14	196		10	100	
14	196	$= \sqrt{\frac{2046}{10} - 201.6}$	10	100	$= \sqrt{\frac{2068}{10} - 196}$
13	169		10	100	
10	100	$= \sqrt{3}$	10	100	$= \sqrt{10.8}$
$\Sigma X = 142$	$\Sigma X^2 = 2046$	$SD = 1.73$	$\Sigma X = 140$	$\Sigma X^2 = 2068$	$SD = 3.29$

approximates the normal curve. If we make the assumption that our data are normally distributed, the SD takes on additional meaning.

In the normal curve shown in Figure 8, the mean is erected vertically from the base line and divides the distribution into two equal parts. In other words, 50% of the scores lie to the left of the mean and 50% to the right. Vertical lines are also erected from the base line corresponding to the different SD units. The mathematics used in placing the SD perpendiculars in the normal curve are beyond the scope of this manual and will not be explained here.

The SD units are so placed that the area (number of scores) between -1 and +1 SD units from the mean corresponds to approximately 68% of the total area. Similarly, 95% of the area lies between -2 and +2 SD units from the mean. Approximately 99% of the cases lie between -3 and +3 SD units from the mean.

Of what value is this information? We can treat our distribution (if we assume that our distribution is approximately normal) in the same way. We can construct a distribution curve for our set of scores and label it in the same way as Figure 9.

As an example, suppose that we have given a test to a large number of students, and we wish to construct a distribution curve from the following information:

Range of scores: 23 to 76

Mean = 50

SD = 10

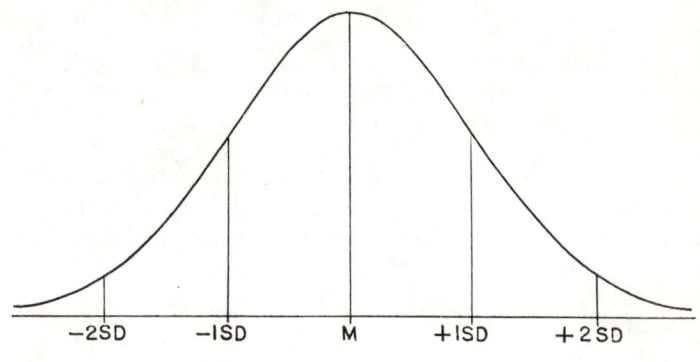

Figure 8

NORMAL CURVE SHOWING MEAN AND SD DISTANCES

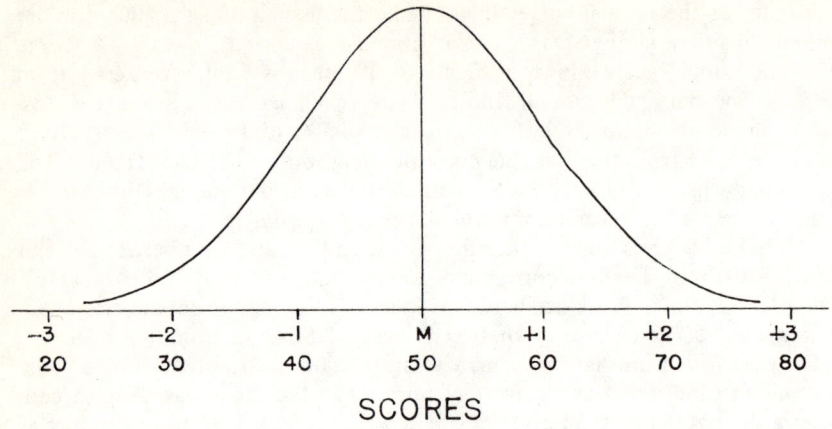

Figure 9

DISTRIBUTION CURVE SHOWING MEAN AND SD UNITS

From the information presented in the distribution curve, we can see at a glance how our scores are spread out and how many scores fall in any particular SD unit. This may be of value in assigning letter grades, A, B, C, D, and F on a class test.

The SD may also be of value in comparing an individual's score on two or more tests. Suppose an individual makes a score of 75 on Test I and 70 on Test II. At a glance we might say that he did better on Test I than on Test II. However, we need more information before we can make a valid comparison.

Suppose that we have the following information:

	Test I	Test II
Individual's Score	75	70
M	60	60
SD	10	5

We cannot compare raw scores from the two different distributions. We must first convert the raw scores to *z scores*, which simply tell us how many SDs the scores are from the mean. To calculate a z score, you subtract the mean from the score and divide by the SD. The formula is:

$$z = \frac{X - M}{SD}$$, where

X is an individual's score
M is the mean
SD is the standard deviation

Test I   Test II
$$z = \frac{75 - 60}{10} = 1.5 \qquad z = \frac{70 - 60}{5} = 2.0$$

Notice that the individual's score on Test II gives a higher z score. We can get an idea of why this happens when we look at the size of the SD for the different tests. For Test II the SD is only 5, while for Test I it is 10. We know that the smaller SD indicates that the distribution is more tightly grouped about the mean than in Test I. Accordingly, his score on Test II in terms of SD units, places him further to the right of the mean than his z score in Test I. This is represented graphically in Figure 10.

A little bit of reasoning shows that a raw score that is below the mean will yield a negative z score. For example, if the individual's score in Test I had been 43, his corresponding z score would have been -1.7.

In order to avoid negative numbers and decimal fractions, other types of scores are sometimes used in place of the z score. One such example is the *T score*.

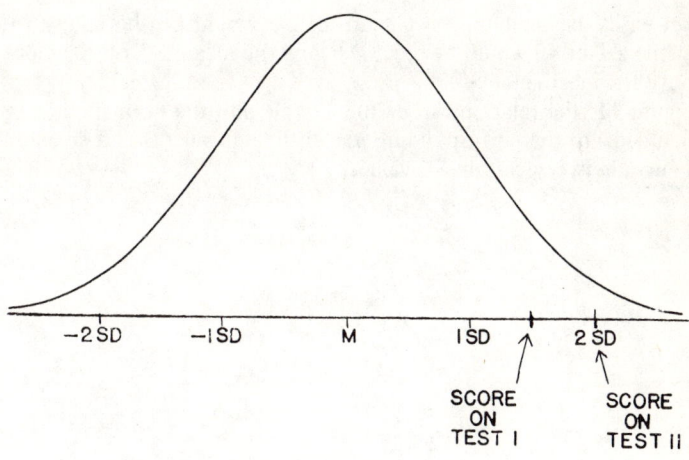

Figure 10

COMPARISON OF TWO STANDARD SCORES

T scores serve the same function as z scores in that they are based on standard deviation distances from the mean. However, they have an additional advantage in that they are always positive in value and are expressed in much larger units. Any z score can be converted to a T score by multiplying the z score by 10 and adding the result to 50. For example, a z score of 1.4 would be a T score of 64; a z of 2.3 would be a T of 73; a z of -1.9 would be a T of 31, etc.

Measures of Variability

Of course, you can go directly from a raw score to a T score. The formula for converting raw scores to T scores would be:

$$T = 50 + \frac{10(X - M)}{SD}$$

Again using the previous example of the individual's raw score of 75 on Test I, we would have:

$$T = 50 + \frac{10(75 - 60)}{10}$$

$$T = 50 + \frac{150}{10}$$

$$T = 50 + 15$$

$$T = 65$$

It can easily be seen that a T score of 50 would be the equivalent of the mean, while a T of 40 would be one SD below the mean, a T of 70 would be two SD's above the mean, etc.

In Figure 11, the relationship of the T scale and the normal curve is shown. Also included are the corresponding percentile equivalents and areas under the normal curve between certain SD values.

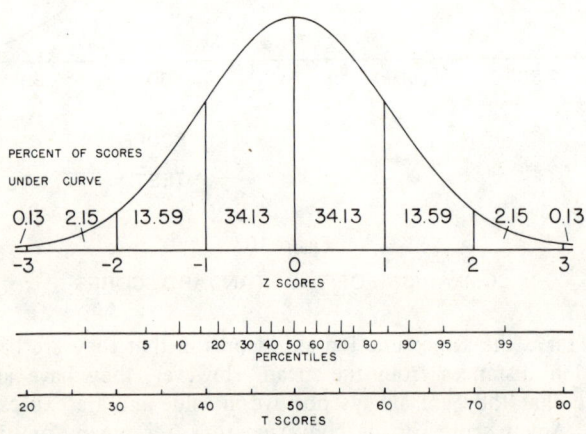

Figure 11

NORMAL CURVE AND DERIVED SCALES

A ROUGH CHECK FOR ACCURACY

From Figures 8, 9, and 11, you can see that the area between M - 3 SD and M + 3 SD just about covers the entire range of scores under the normal curve, since 99% of the distribution lies between -3 and +3 SD units. We can use this fact to exercise a rough check on the accuracy of our calculations of the SD for a group of scores. For an approximately normal distribution, the SD should be about one-sixth of the range, *when N is quite large.*

When working with only 50 or 100 scores, however, you will find that the SD is about one-fourth or one-fifth of the range. So, if you calculated the SD for a distribution containing 72 scores where the lowest score is 25 and the highest is 88, you would find that the range is 88 - 25 = 63. Accordingly, you would expect the calculated SD to be in the vicinity of 13 to 16, since one-fifth of 63 is 13 and one-fourth of 63 is about 16. If your calculated SD turned out to be 2.67 or 29.76, you would probably want to recheck your work for possible errors. This technique will not work every time, because some distributions will have peculiar, nonnormal shapes; but for most situations the one-fourth to one-fifth rule of thumb will be helpful.

CALCULATION OF THE STANDARD DEVIATION FROM GROUPED DATA

We noted earlier that there are times when it is convenient to be able to calculate the mean, the median, and percentiles from data that have already been grouped into a frequency distribution. This section describes how the standard deviation also can be calculated from grouped data. It might be a good idea to review the technique for calculating the mean from grouped data, which was

Table 21

CALCULATION OF THE SD FOR BIOLOGY SCORES, GROUPED DATA

Scores	f	d	fd	fd^2
85-89	1	3	3	9
80-84	3	2	6	12
75-79	6	1	6 (+15)	6
70-74	15	0		
65-69	12	-1	-12	12
60-64	8	-2	-16	32
55-59	3	-3	- 9	27
50-54	2	-4	- 8 (-45)	32
N = 50			Σfd = -30	Σfd^2 = 130

illustrated in Table 11 in Chapter 3. Table 21 shows the same distribution of biology scores used to illustrate the computation of the mean in Table 11, except that a new column, fd^2, has been added.

After you have completed the steps described earlier in the calculation of the mean, it is only necessary to compute the entries in the fd^2 column. To obtain each fd^2 entry, multiply each fd by the corresponding d value. In Table 21, $3 \times 3 = 9$, $2 \times 6 = 12$, etc., for the rest of the distribution. Remember, fd^2 means $fd \times d$, NOT $fd \times fd$. For example, the entry in the 80-84 interval is $2 \times 6 = 12$, not $6 \times 6 = 36$. Also note that all the entries in the fd^2 column are positive. There are no negative numbers, because multiplying a negative d by a negative fd results in a positive answer. For example, in the 55-59 interval, $-3 \times -9 = 27$.

The next step is to add the fd^2 column to obtain $\Sigma fd^2 = 130$.

The formula for the SD from grouped data is:

$$SD = i \sqrt{\frac{N\Sigma fd^2 - (\Sigma fd)^2}{N^2}}, \text{ where}$$

i is the size of the interval
N is the number of scores
Σfd^2 is the sum of the fd^2 column
Σfd is the sum of the fd column

For the frequency distribution of Table 21:

$$SD = 5 \sqrt{\frac{50(130) - (-30)^2}{(50)^2}}$$

$$= 5 \sqrt{\frac{6500 - 900}{2500}}$$

$$= 5 \sqrt{\frac{5600}{2500}}$$

$$= 5 \sqrt{2.24}$$

$$= 5 (1.5)$$

$$SD = 7.5$$

Some of the textbooks in measurement have a slightly different formula for the SD, showing N outside the square root sign, instead of N^2 underneath the square root sign.

PROBLEMS

1. For the following quiz scores, calculate the SD by the two methods described in the text.

   Deviation Method

X	x	x^2
11		
10		
9		
9		
8		
7		
6		
6		
5		
4		

   a. $SD = \sqrt{\dfrac{\Sigma x^2}{N}} =$

Measures of Variability

Whole Score Method

X	X²
11	
10	
9	
9	
8	
7	
6	
6	
5	
4	

b. $SD = \sqrt{\dfrac{\Sigma X^2}{N} - M^2} =$

c. Which method did you find easier? Which method would be easier to use if the scores were small and the mean were a whole number?

2. For the following distribution of scores on a history test, calculate the SD using any method of calculation that you prefer.

$\underline{X}$

20

19

18

18

17

17

17

17

16

16

15

15

14

11

<u>10</u>

3. Judy Jones takes a test in an algebra course and an English course. The following information is taken from the two tests:

	Algebra	English
Judy's score	56	68
Mean	50	60
SD	3	5

a. In terms of z scores, on which test did she do better?

b. Convert her z scores to T scores.

c. Paul Peterson received a score of 47 on the same algebra test. What was his z score? What was his T score?

4. A short quiz was given to 20 home economics students.

X
16
13
13
12
12
12
11
11
11
11
11
10
10
10
8
7
6
6
5
5

a. Calculate the mean, the median, the mode, and the SD.

Mean =

Median =

Mode =

SD =

b. If this small sample is normally distributed, 68% of the scores should fall between what two values?

_____ and _____.

5. The following data are 30 scores on a biology quiz.

25	16	13
25	16	12
23	15	12
22	15	11
20	15	11
19	15	10
19	15	9
18	14	8
18	14	7
17	14	2

Calculate the mean, the median, the mode, and the SD.

Mean =

Median =

Mode =

SD =

6. A test was administered to 100 members of a college sociology class. Use *grouped data* formulas for calculating the necessary statistics.

Scores	f
50-54	3
45-49	7
40-44	14
35-39	15
30-34	24
25-29	16
20-24	13
15-19	6
10-14	2
	N = 100

Calculate the mean and the SD.

Mean =

SD =

Measures of Variability

7. A group of 90 seniors is given a vocational aptitude test with the following results. Calculate the mean, the median, the mode, and the SD.

Scores	f
23-25	4
20-22	9
17-19	16
14-16	24
11-13	20
8-10	12
5-7	3
2-4	2
	N = 90

Mean =

Median =

Mode =

SD =

Chapter 6

CORRELATION

The previous chapters have been concerned with only one distribution of scores. We examined, for example, how a measure of central tendency or a measure of variability gave us some information about a distribution of scores. In this chapter, however, we will be concerned about the *relationship* of *two* distributions.

At one time or another we've probably all heard questions such as, "What's the relationship between high-school performance and college success?" or "What's the relationship between intelligence and reading ability?" or "What's the relationship between college entrance exam scores and college performance?" These questions and many similar ones can be answered by a statistical method called *correlation*.

An example might help to clarify the concept of correlation. Let us suppose that we are interested in seeing if there is a relationship between athletic ability and scholastic ability. Is a superior athlete a superior student, a poor student, or just average? To test our hypothesis we will choose five college football players and see how well they are doing academically. (Obviously, we would want more than five subjects in an actual experiment, but such a small number will serve for our illustration.)

We then have the coach rank these five players on their overall ability, and we also rank them in terms of their grade-point average (GPA). Table 22 shows the results of our experiment.

Table 22

ILLUSTRATION OF PERFECT POSITIVE CORRELATION

Player	Rank on Football Ability	Rank on GPA
A	1	1
B	2	2
C	3	3
D	4	4
E	5	5

Notice that A was the best football player and also the best student, B was second best at both, and so on down to E, who was the poorest player and the worst student. This is an illustration of *perfect positive correlation*. It is *perfect* because there are no reversals or changes from the 1-1, 2-2, 3-3, 4-4, 5-5 pairs of ranks, and it is *positive* because both variables increase together. If you are high in one you are high in the other, and if you are low in one you are low in the other. Perfect positive correlation is denoted by a coefficient of +1.00.

Let us suppose that our little experiment turned out in just the opposite way, and the rankings on football ability and GPA turned out to be as shown in Table 23.

Table 23

ILLUSTRATION OF PERFECT NEGATIVE CORRELATION

Player	Rank on Football Ability	Rank on GPA
A	1	5
B	2	4
C	3	3
D	4	2
E	5	1

As you can see, there is a definite relationship shown here, but in just the opposite direction. Player A, who is the best at football, has the worst GPA, and so on down to E, who is the worst player but the best student. This is an illustration of *perfect negative correlation*. It is *perfect* because there are no reversals or changes from the best-worst, second best-second worst, etc. pairs of ranks, and it is *negative* because as one variable increases, the other decreases. The better you are at football, the poorer you are at getting grades. Perfect negative correlation is denoted by a coefficient of -1.00.

And, of course, it is possible that there would be no relationship between football ability and GPA. Player A might rank first on one and third on the other, while player B was fifth on one and third on the other. In other words, there is no pattern of relationship shown in the data. This would be zero correlation, and the coefficient would simply be zero, indicating no relationship.

We have listed the extreme cases, where the coefficient of correlation was either 1.00 or -1.00 or zero. Actually, we should think of correlation coefficients on a continuum: they can vary from -1.00 to 1.00.

For example, the correlation between height and weight might be .70. What does .70 indicate to us? Any coefficient less than 1.00 means that there have been some reversals or changes in the relative ranking. In Table 22, for example, suppose that on GPA player C ranked fourth and D ranked third. This would result in a coefficient that was less than 1.00, but it would still be quite high and still positive, maybe around .80. We would still say that the relationship in Table 22 was positive and "high." In other words, those that were good players "tended to be" good scholars, and those that were poor players "in general" were poor scholars. As there get to be more and more reversals in the relative ranks, we find that the correlation gets lower and lower. If the relationship between height and weight is .70, this would indicate that in general, taller people are heavier, and shorter people are lighter—but there are a goodly number of reversals, with some tall, skinny, light people and some short, stocky, heavy people.

In summary, there are two important characteristics to keep in mind when evaluating a correlation coefficient. We must observe the *sign* of the coefficient and the *size* of the coefficient. If the sign is *positive* we know that as one variable increases, so does the other. Thus, if the relationship between height and weight or high-school and college performance is positive, we would know that tall people tend to be heavier than short people or that students who did well in high school will do better in college than their low-achieving classmates. If the sign is *negative* we know that as one variable increases the other decreases. Thus, if the relationship between coordination and age for people over 40 is negative, we know that the older one is, the poorer is his coordination.

The *size* of the coefficient, as we mentioned earlier, indicates the *amount* of the relationship. As was pointed out in Tables 22 and 23, when there are no changes or reversals in ranks in the two variables, the coefficient is 1.00. As there get to be more and more changes in the relative rankings, the coefficient becomes lower and lower until it finally reaches zero, with no relationship between the two variables.

Another way of looking at correlation is by means of a *scattergram*. A scattergram is simply a graph showing the plotted pairs of values of the two variables being studied. For example, let us suppose that we would like to determine the relationship of height and weight among male college students, and we select a random sample of 20 students. We measure their height and weight and list them in pairs on a chart similar to Table 24.

A scattergram can now be constructed by plotting the 20 paired values on a graph, as shown in Figure 12. In examining Figure 12 you would expect that the correlation would be positive (those with greater heights tend to weigh more) and quite high. However, the correlation certainly isn't perfect, since you can find a number of reversals—student #16, for example, is 3 inches taller than student #9, but weighs 6 pounds less! The actual coefficient in Table 24 and Figure 12 is .81, which is quite high.

Although a scattergram can tell us something about the relationship between two variables, we still need a precise mathematical technique that will yield a single value that tells us instantly the extent of the correlation. Such a single

Table 24

WEIGHTS AND HEIGHTS OF 20 COLLEGE STUDENTS

Student #	Weight	Height	Student #	Weight	Height
1	177	70	11	147	64
2	174	69	12	162	70
3	190	72	13	177	70
4	174	70	14	147	65
5	177	72	15	180	72
6	162	67	16	153	69
7	186	71	17	168	68
8	165	67	18	150	68
9	159	66	19	168	71
10	171	70	20	159	69

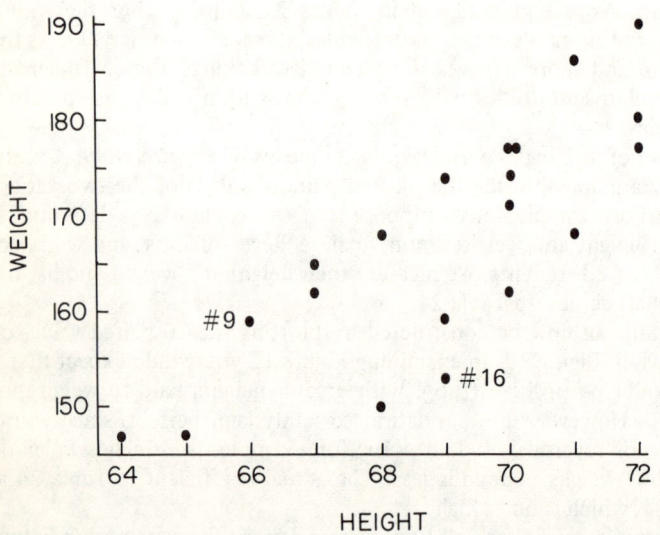

Figure 12

SCATTERGRAM OF HEIGHTS AND WEIGHTS

value is called the *correlation coefficient*—sort of an index number which indicates how much of a relationship exists between the two variables and whether the relationship is positive or negative.

There are a large number of statistical techniques which are used to compute a correlation coefficient, but we will be concerned with the computational techniques of only two. They are the Spearman rank-difference method and the Pearson product-moment method; their coefficients are denoted by r_s and r, respectively. The remainder of this chapter will be devoted to computational techniques, and the next chapter will apply the techniques to test construction and evaluation.

SPEARMAN RANK-DIFFERENCE METHOD

One way in which we can determine the relationship between two sets of scores is by computing a correlation coefficient on the basis of the ranks of the individuals. This method is called the rank-difference method. We need to rank each one of the individuals on both tests, obtain the difference in rank, square the differences, sum these differences, and substitute in the following formula.

$$r_s = 1 - \frac{6\Sigma D^2}{N(N^2-1)}, \text{ where}$$

r_s is the correlation coefficient (older texts use the symbol ρ)
ΣD^2 is the sum of the squared differences in the two ranks
N is the number of individuals

Table 25 shows the results of two tests taken by 10 students. Let us say that Test I is an algebra test and Test II is a geometry test. Since both tests are measuring mathematical ability, we would expect that the results should agree quite well—in other words the *correlation* between the two tests should be high. Let us use this example as an illustration of the rank-difference method for calculating a correlation coefficient.

$$N = 10$$
$$N^2 = 100$$
$$r_s = 1 - \frac{6\Sigma D^2}{N(N^2-1)}$$
$$= 1 - \frac{6(19.5)}{10(100-1)}$$
$$= 1 - \frac{117}{990}$$
$$= 1 - .118$$
$$r_s = .882 \text{ or } .88$$

The steps in the computation of the rank-difference method are:
1. Divide the sheet into seven columns labeled: Individual; X_1 (score on Test I); R_1 (rank on Test I); X_2 (score on Test II); R_2 (rank on Test II); D (difference in ranks); and D^2 (difference squared).
2. Place the score for each individual in the appropriate columns.
3. Rank these scores on the basis of the highest score as Rank 1, and so forth for both tests.
4. Obtain the difference by subtracting R_1 from R_2 and place in the D column.
5. Square each one of these differences and place in the D^2 column.
6. Sum the D^2 column to obtain ΣD^2 and substitute in the formula.
7. The denominator is always the quantity $N(N^2-1)$. To find this quantity, square N, subtract 1 from N^2, and multiply by N.
8. Perform the division indicated by $\dfrac{6\Sigma D^2}{N(N^2-1)}$ and subtract the quotient from 1. This figure is the correlation coefficient.

Notice in the formula $r_s = 1 - \dfrac{6\Sigma D^2}{N(N^2-1)}$ that the size of the rank differences directly affects the size of the coefficient. If the correlation is perfect, that is, if the ranks are the same for both tests, each rank difference in the D column will equal zero, and the corresponding D^2 column will also be zero. This makes the numerator of the fraction zero, and thus the quotient is zero. As a result, the correlation is 1.00. As the relationship between the scores becomes poorer, the rank differences increase and the fraction to be subtracted from 1 becomes larger. In the case where there is a negative correlation, rank differences are very

Table 25

ILLUSTRATION OF RANK-DIFFERENCE METHOD

Individual	Test I		Test II		Difference	Difference^2
	X_1	R_1	X_2	R_2	D	D^2
A	18	1	24	2	1	1
B	17	2	27	1	1	1
C	14	3	17	6	3	9
D	13	4.5	22	3	1.5	2.25
E	13	4.5	19	5	.5	.25
F	12	6	20	4	2	4
G	11	7	14	7	0	0
H	9	8	11	8	0	0
I	7	9	3	10	1	1
J	5	10	6	9	1	1
					$\Sigma D^2 =$	19.5

large and the fraction is greater than 1. Obviously the resulting subtraction results in a negative coefficient.

In Test I in Table 25, individuals D and E both made the same score. When scores are tied, it would be incorrect to give the two scores different ranks. We must give the two tied scores the same rank which falls directly between the preceding score and the following score. For example, if there are scores of 9, 8, 8, and 6, there is a tie for second and third ranks, and we assign the average rank of 2.5 to both scores of 8. If three scores are tied, we use the same method. For example, with scores of 9, 8, 8, 8, and 6, there is a tie for the second, third, and fourth ranks, and we assign the average rank of 3 to each of the three scores of 8.

The coefficient that we obtained in Table 25 is +.88. This is indicative of a high positive correlation in the two sets of scores. This correlation is based on the rank differences in these two sets of scores. The rank-difference method can be used on measurements that are of the ordinal type or above.

In the next section we will consider a method of obtaining a correlation coefficient which does not use the ranks of the scores but utilizes the actual sizes of the scores in the computation. This is called the Pearson product-moment method, and the coefficient is called the Pearson r.

PEARSON PRODUCT-MOMENT r

The Pearson r is probably the most widely used method of correlation, and this coefficient will show up in your reading on many different occasions. The formula for calculating the Pearson r is:

$$r = \frac{\frac{\Sigma XY}{N} - M_x M_y}{SD_x SD_y} \text{, where}$$

> r is the correlation coefficient
> N is the number of *pairs* of scores
> ΣXY is the sum of the products of each person's *pair* of scores
> M_x is the mean of the X values
> M_y is the mean of the Y values
> SD_x is the standard deviation of the X values
> SD_y is the standard deviation of the Y values

Let us take a look at this somewhat complex formula. You are familiar with most of these terms from previous chapters. SD_x and SD_y are simply the standard deviations of the two distributions, M_x and M_y are their corresponding means, and N is the number of pairs of observations.

The only new term is ΣXY, which is the sum of the products of each person's pair of scores. For example, in Table 26, the XY product for A is 14 × 12 = 168; for B it is 17 × 11 = 187, etc. The sum of this column, ΣXY, is 1196.

Table 26 below shows the results of a manual dexterity test (X) and a steadiness test (Y) for 10 pupils. Is there any relation between the two tests?

Correlation

Table 26

ILLUSTRATION OF PEARSON PRODUCT-MOMENT r

Individual	X	Y	X^2	Y^2	XY
A	14	12	196	144	168
B	17	11	289	121	187
C	15	9	225	81	135
D	13	9	169	81	117
E	12	9	144	81	108
F	12	8	144	64	96
G	14	11	196	121	154
H	12	6	144	36	72
I	11	9	121	81	99
J	10	6	100	36	60
	130	90	1728	846	1196

Calculations:

$$M_x = \frac{130}{10} = 13 \qquad M_y = \frac{90}{10} = 9$$

$$SD_x = \sqrt{\frac{\Sigma X^2}{N} - M^2} \qquad SD_y = \sqrt{\frac{\Sigma Y^2}{N} - M^2}$$

$$= \sqrt{\frac{1728}{10} - (13)^2} \qquad = \sqrt{\frac{846}{10} - (9)^2}$$

$$= \sqrt{172.8 - 169} \qquad = \sqrt{84.6 - 81}$$

$$= \sqrt{3.8} \qquad = \sqrt{3.6}$$

$$SD_x = 1.9 \qquad SD_y = 1.9$$

Substitution:

$$r = \frac{\frac{\Sigma XY}{N} - M_x M_y}{SD_x SD_y} = \frac{\frac{1196}{10} - (13)(9)}{(1.9)(1.9)}$$

$$= \frac{119.6 - 117}{3.61} = \frac{2.6}{3.61}$$

$$r = .72$$

Since an r of .72 is quite high, we would say that these two tests seem to be measuring the same skill.

The steps in the calculation of the Pearson r are:
1. Divide the sheet into six columns labeled:
   Individual; X (score on Test X); Y (score on Test Y); X^2 (square of the X score); Y^2 (square of the Y score); and XY (product of each pair of X and Y scores).
2. Enter each individual's score for both tests in the appropriate columns. Sum these columns to find ΣX and ΣY.
3. Square each X score and place the X^2 value in that column. Also square each Y score and place the Y^2 value in that column. Sum these columns to obtain ΣX^2 and ΣY^2.
4. Multiply each X by its corresponding Y to obtain XY and enter in the XY column. Sum this column to obtain ΣXY.
5. Calculate the mean and standard deviation for both X and Y.
6. Substitute in the formula for the Pearson r.

The Pearson r is interpreted in the same way as the coefficient for the rank-difference method. The Pearson r can be calculated on measurements that are of the interval type or ratio type.

COMPARISON OF THE TWO METHODS

We have discussed two types of correlation that yield measures of relationship. Which one should be used?

As you have noted, the Pearson product-moment method utilizes the actual size of the scores, while the rank-difference method deals only with the location of the scores in a series and makes no allowances for the size of the gaps between scores. Individuals who score 75, 74, and 50 on a test might receive ranks of 1, 2, and 3. Notice that there is only one score interval between 75 and 74, and the ranks would be 1 and 2. However, there is a wide gap between 74 and 50, yet the score 50 would receive a rank of 3. Much accuracy may be lost in converting scores to ranks, especially when the scores are tied. The Pearson product-moment r is to be preferred for greater accuracy. However, the rank-difference method has its uses. Since it is easily computed, it is a handy preliminary device to check for the presence of a relationship. It is also useful in discovering relationships in criteria that can not be dimensionalized. For example, we may want to find out if any relationship exists between scores on an achievement test and excellence in extracurricular activities. We can hardly assign scores to extracurricular activities, but we could have several instructors judge performances on extracurricular activities and rank each individual. We could then obtain a correlation between these ranks and the ranks of test scores on the achievement test. In situations like this, the rank-difference method has its greatest value.

CORRELATION AND SAMPLE SIZE

The confidence that we can put in our correlation coefficient is directly related to the number of pairs of scores on which it is based. If we want to see, for example, what the correlation is between IQ test score and reading ability, we would not be content with only 15 or 20 pairs of scores, but we would probably want several hundred students taking both tests. In the examples used in this chapter and in the problems to follow, N has been small in order to simplify the computations. In actual practice most correlation studies involve hundreds of examinees. The reader is referred to any current statistics text for further discussion on the effect of sample size on correlation.

CALCULATION OF THE PEARSON r FROM GROUPED DATA

Several current textbooks in the field of tests and measurements include a computational technique using grouped data in computing the Pearson r. The technique is very time-consuming, and this author feels that if a student has access to a calculator or even an adding machine, the whole score method for the Pearson r presented in this chapter will be faster and less subject to error. However, if you need to know the grouped data technique, you can consult one of the current tests-and-measurements textbooks.

PROBLEMS

1. Ten students are given a unit test in chemistry and a short algebra quiz. Use the rank-difference method to calculate the correlation coefficient.

Student	Chemistry	R_1	Algebra	R_2	D	D^2
A	67		44			
B	55		12			
C	44		53			
D	32		60			
E	22		25			
F	21		10			
G	19		11			
H	17		9			
I	11		8			
J	4		6			

$\Sigma D^2 =$

a. $r_s = 1 - \dfrac{6\Sigma D^2}{N(N^2-1)} =$

b. What does this coefficient indicate about the two tests?

2. A teacher of physical education wished to know if there was any relationship between performance in gymnastics and wrestling ability among physical education majors. He ranked 10 majors on gymnastics (R_1), and the wrestling coach ranked the same majors on proficiency in wrestling (R_2). From these ranks, determine the coefficient of correlation by the rank-difference method.

Student	R_1	R_2	D	D^2
AB	6	4		
CD	4	2		
KL	1	6		
ST	7	5		
EF	10	8		
OP	9	9		
GH	2	3		
IJ	3	7		
QR	5	10		
MN	8	1		

$\Sigma D^2 =$

a. $r_s = 1 - \dfrac{6\Sigma D^2}{N(N^2-1)}$

b. Are gymnastic ability and wrestling ability related?

Correlation

3. A vocabulary test (X) and a spelling test (Y) are given to 10 sixth-graders. Calculate the Pearson r for the scores on the two tests below.

Pupil	X	Y	X^2	Y^2	XY
A	16	21			
B	15	18			
C	12	22			
D	12	17			
E	9	18			
F	9	15			
G	8	15			
H	7	12			
I	6	11			
J	6	11			
	100	160			

a. $M_x =$ $\qquad$ $M_y =$

b. $SD_x =$ $\qquad$ $SD_y =$

c. $r = \dfrac{\dfrac{\Sigma XY}{N} - M_x M_y}{SD_x SD_y}$

d. Do the two tests show a high degree of relationship?

4. Short quizzes in music history (X) and automotive mechanics (Y) are administered to 10 students. Calculate a Pearson r for these data.

Student	X	Y	X^2	Y^2	XY
WJB	14	4			
ARD	12	3			
ANF	10	4			
SGG	10	6			
JDH	9	7			
KJH	8	10			
DRM	8	7			
CEN	8	9			
LWS	7	13			
APT	4	17			
	90	80			

Correlation

a. $M_x =$ $\qquad$ $M_y =$

b. $SD_x =$ $\qquad$ $SD_y =$

c. $r = \dfrac{\dfrac{\Sigma XY}{N} - M_x M_y}{SD_x SD_y} =$

d. What does such a relationship show?

5. A teacher at a vocational school administers a clerical ability test (X) and a filing test (Y) to 20 secretarial students.

Student	X	Y	Student	X	Y
A	14	13	K	8	10
B	14	13	L	8	10
C	6	9	M	15	13
D	19	18	N	12	12
E	13	11	O	9	11
F	7	9	P	16	16
G	15	15	Q	11	10
H	14	13	R	15	17
I	14	12	S	11	11
J	17	18	T	16	17

a. On a sheet of graph paper, plot a scattergram of the above data.

b. From the scattergram alone, what can you say about these two tests?

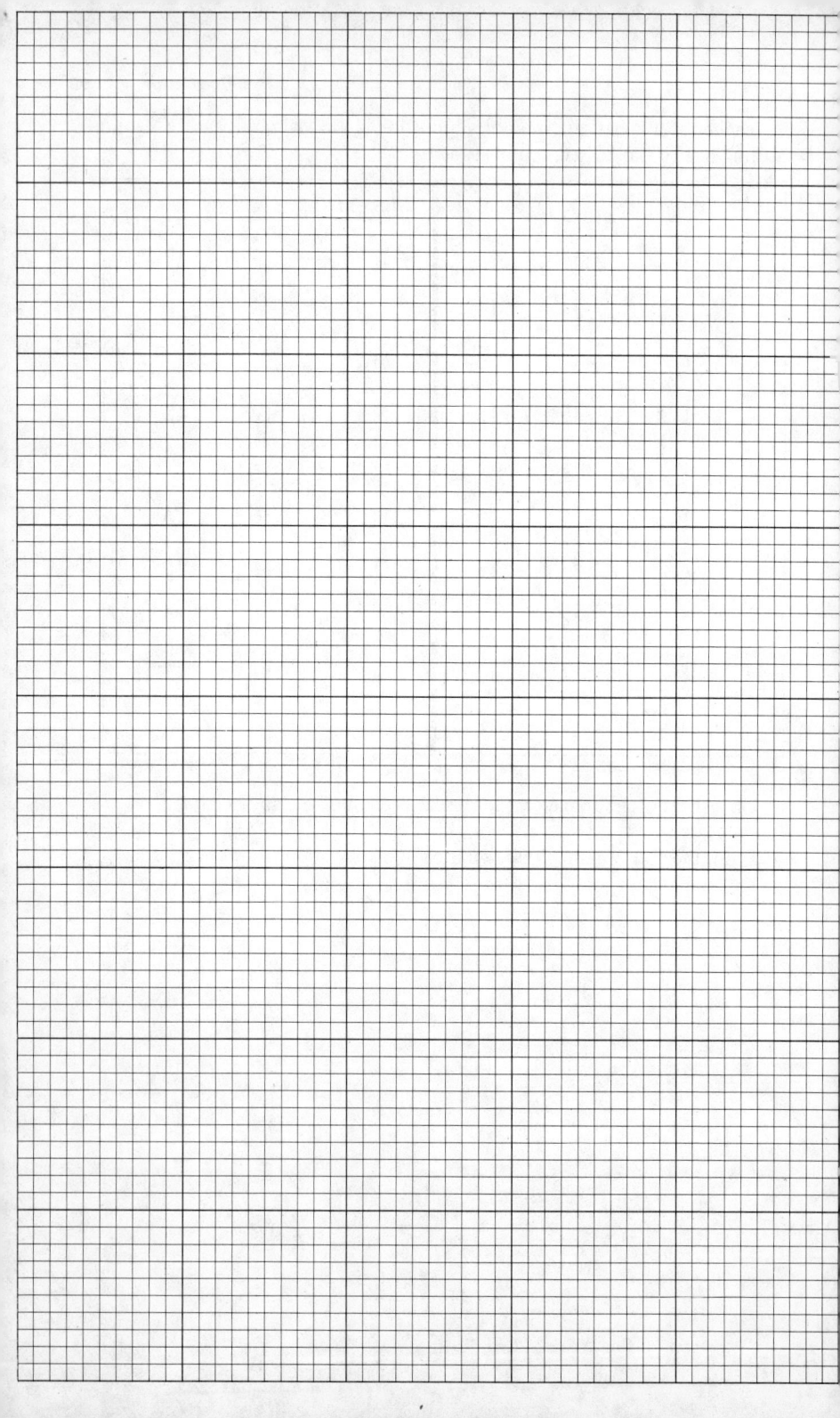

Chapter 7

EVALUATION AND INTERPRETATION OF TESTS

Finally, we have come to the point where we can devote a discussion to some of the construction procedures used by test publishers in standardized tests. The statistical methods presented in the previous chapters form a foundation for the procedures to be outlined in this chapter. Because of the introductory nature of this manual, we will have to omit some of the more technical topics, but any discussion of test construction must treat the concepts of *reliability* and *validity*.

RELIABILITY

One important characteristic of any measuring device, be it a bathroom scale or a reading readiness test, is its *reliability*. That is, we expect the measurements yielded by any instrument to be *consistent* or *repeatable*. If Johnny's weight as taken at 1-hour intervals on the same scale were 75, 98, and 36 pounds, or his IQ scores as measured at 1-month intervals by the same test were 126, 180, and 92, we would seriously doubt the reliability of the bathroom scale and the particular IQ test. We expect a reliable instrument to give us consistent results. We do not, of course, expect to get *identical* results each time we measure some human characteristic more than once, because most instruments are not perfectly reliable, but we do expect a certain degree of "sameness" in our measurements.

It does not take a great deal of imagination to see that the methods of correlation discussed in Chapter 6 could be used to determine the reliability of a test. If we gave the same test twice to the same group of students, we would expect a high positive correlation if the test were reliable. If the measurements were consistent, those pupils who scored high on one administration of the test would tend to score high on the second administration, and those scoring low the first time should also score low the second time. The coefficient of correlation, the Pearson r, for example, would be a direct indicator of the amount of reliability. If r were high, it would indicate a great degree of consistency between the two administrations of the test. If some students who scored high on the first testing scored low on the second, the value of r would be lower, indicating a lower degree of reliability.

However, determining the reliability of a test is not quite as simple as it may first appear, and a number of special methods have been developed. We will consider three general methods often used by test writers and publishers to determine the reliability of their tests—the test-retest, the parallel forms, and the internal consistency methods.

Test-Retest Method

The simplest and most straightforward method for determining reliability would be to give the test twice to the same group of individuals. We could then use the Pearson r to determine the correlation between the two administrations of the test. As we noted earlier, the coefficient of correlation yielded by this method would indicate the amount of relationship. If r were high, the measurements would be consistent and the test would be considered reliable.

Despite its simplicity, there are a number of problems involved in the test-retest method. If the test is repeated within a short time interval, many individuals might be able to recall answers that they had given previously and could spend more time on the more difficult material. Not all individuals would do this, of course, so this would increase some scores and not others and would lower the coefficient of correlation. The type of test would determine the amount of transfer from one test administration to the next.

On the other hand, if the time interval between the initial administration of the test and its repetition is too long, growth and maturity (especially if the examinees are children) would affect performance on the second administration. Certain experiences by different individuals during this interval might influence their performance also—again tending to lower the correlation coefficient.

Because of the difficulty in controlling these conditions, the test-retest method is not often used. It is always included in a discussion of reliability, however, since it *defines* the term. Theoretically, a reliable test should always give consistent results from one administration to the next.

Parallel Forms Method

One obvious way to avoid the practice effect of the test-retest method for short time intervals would be to use another form of the same test. This parallel forms method (also called alternate forms or comparable forms) means that a test author would have to write twice as many items as would be needed for just a single test and that the items would be randomly assigned to either Form A or Form B. Both forms of the test are then given to a sample of individuals. A time interval of 5 days to 2 weeks might separate the two administrations, but there should be very little practice effect since the two forms contain completely different items. The reliability of the test is given by the Pearson r calculated between the two sets of test scores.

When accurate parallel forms have been constructed (such as Form L and Form M of one of the earlier editions of the Stanford-Binet IQ test), they have provided a very useful research tool and a defensible definition of reliability. Nevertheless, it is imperative to keep in mind that the use of parallel forms does not really eliminate the problem of growth or maturity over longer time intervals that we encountered in the test-retest method. As individuals change, so do their responses to an identical item or to a completely different item that is testing the same content. What the use of parallel forms does do is eliminate the *need* for long time intervals between two administrations of a test.

The greatest drawback to the parallel forms method lies in the sheer amount of labor required for an author to construct the parallel form. Writing good items for one test is a difficult task (as you may have learned in a tests-and-measurements course), and writing twice as many is a real problem. There may be a number of occasions when we would like to determine the reliability of a test we have constructed for classroom purposes but when the extra time and effort involved would prevent us from using the parallel forms approach.

Internal Consistency Methods

The two methods described above are similar in that they both involve *two* administrations—either of the same test or of parallel forms. However, methods involving *internal consistency* are based on a *single* administration of the test. The test is then divided into two parts (e.g., two subsections, with random assignment of items into the two parts), and a correlation coefficient is calculated between the two portions of the test. Obviously, this correlation coefficient has a different interpretation from the coefficient for the test-retest and parallel forms methods: it describes *internal consistency*.

One commonly used technique for breaking the test into two parts in order to determine internal consistency is the *odd-even method*. With this method, each individual has two scores—a score on the odd-numbered items in a test and a score on the even-numbered items. It is necessary to go through the answer sheet for each individual and tabulate the number of items correct on the odd items and the number correct on the even items. The scores are then placed in the familiar X and Y columns of the Pearson product-moment method, as shown in Table 27. In essence, we are treating the two halves as separate tests. The tabulation for one individual might be:

Individual	Total Score	Odd-numbered Items Correct	Even-numbered Items Correct	X (Odd)	Y (Even)
A	32	17	15	17	15

We would do this for each individual in the test until we had a table similar to Table 27. The coefficient yielded by this method would be the relationship of the two halves of the test. However, we want a coefficient that gives us the reliability of the entire test. It is necessary to substitute in the following formula (Spearman-Brown prophecy formula).

$$r_t = \frac{2r_{oe}}{1 + r_{oe}}, \text{ where}$$

r_t is the reliability coefficient of the entire test
r_{oe} is the coefficient of correlation between the two halves

The r_t is the reliability coefficient of the entire test. Let us consider the example shown in Table 27, using this method for finding the reliability of a test.

Evaluation and Interpretation of Tests

Table 27

ILLUSTRATION OF ODD-EVEN METHOD FOR DETERMINING RELIABILITY

Pupil	X (Odd)	Y (Even)	X^2	Y^2	XY
A	12	10	144	100	120
B	10	8	100	64	80
C	9	11	81	121	99
D	14	11	196	121	154
E	13	10	169	100	130
F	8	8	64	64	64
G	12	11	144	121	132
H	11	10	121	100	110
I	11	11	121	121	121
J	10	10	100	100	100
	110	100	1240	1012	1110

Calculations:

$$M_x = \frac{110}{10} = 11 \qquad M_y = \frac{100}{10} = 10$$

$$SD_x = \sqrt{\frac{\Sigma X^2}{N} - M_x^2} \qquad SD_y = \sqrt{\frac{\Sigma Y^2}{N} - M_y^2}$$

$$= \sqrt{\frac{1240}{10} - (11)^2} \qquad = \sqrt{\frac{1012}{10} - (10)^2}$$

$$= \sqrt{124 - 121} \qquad = \sqrt{101.2 - 100}$$

$$= \sqrt{3} \qquad = \sqrt{1.2}$$

$$SD_x = 1.7 \qquad SD_y = 1.1$$

Substitution:

$$r_{oe} = \frac{\frac{\Sigma XY}{N} - M_x M_y}{SD_x SD_y} = \frac{\frac{1110}{10} - (11)(10)}{(1.7)(1.1)}$$

$$= \frac{111 - 110}{1.87} = \frac{1}{1.87}$$

$$r_{oe} = .53$$

The steps in determining the reliability of the two halves of the test are the same as in the general procedure for determining the Pearson product-moment r. However, the coefficient yielded is based on one-half of the test. To find the reliability of the entire test, it is necessary to substitute in the Spearman-Brown prophecy formula.

The reliability of the entire test is given by:

$$r_t = \frac{2r_{oe}}{1 + r_{oe}}$$

$$= \frac{2(.53)}{1 + .53}$$

$$= \frac{1.06}{1.53}$$

$$r_t = .69$$

But what is the rationale for the odd-even method of determining reliability? The test-retest and parallel forms methods were straightforward: if the test were reliable, an individual would make comparable scores relative to the rest of the group on both administrations. Is there similar reasoning behind the odd-even method (and other internal consistency methods)? When we separate an individual's total score into odd and even correct, we expect to see similar results on the odd and even items (if odd and even items are of similar difficulty) relative to the rest of the group. If this is the case, the test is reliable; that is, its measurements are consistent. If the individual does not do equally well on the odd and even halves, the test is not measuring consistently and, therefore, is not reliable. However, this "split-half" method for determining reliability is not measuring the same concept as the test-retest and parallel forms methods. It measures internal consistency and not consistency from administration to administration.

The split-half method should not be used on what are termed "speed tests." Theoretically, most tests are timed tests, in that a student does not have an infinite amount of time to complete them. But a speed test, strictly speaking, is one where every examinee would get *all* the items correct if enough time were allowed. Obviously, this would lead to problems with internal consistency, since every examinee would have the same score (i.e., 100% correct) on each half.

Comparing the Three Methods

The test-retest, parallel forms, and internal consistency methods for estimating the reliability of a test will result in different estimates for the same test. This does not surprise us, since we know that there are specific characteristics that are unique to each method. For example, we have already noted that the test-retest method can be affected by practice and lengthy time intervals, the parallel forms method is sensitive to lengthy time intervals, and internal consistency methods are different from stability (test-retest) or equivalency (parallel forms) methods. In fact, split-half reliability coefficients tend to be higher than those obtained by either of the other two methods. For these reasons, it is important that the method used be cited in test manuals and journal articles, so the reader can interpret the results correctly.

Since all the methods have their shortcomings, is there any one method that is preferred? The answer to this question lies in the purpose of the investigator. Since the test-retest approach has limited use because of the practice effect, we are often left with a choice between parallel forms or internal consistency methods. If the investigator is involved in test theory—for example, development of alternative methods for estimating reliability, or effect of test length or item difficulty on reliability—he or she will probably choose one of the internal consistency methods. On the other hand, the *test user* (clinical psychologist, educational consultant) might be more interested in a parallel forms approach, since he or she may be running *before* and *after* studies where the same test is given a second time but in a different form.

We are likely to see both methods cited frequently in the literature; however, the fact that internal consistency tests are well suited for computer analysis makes them very desirable. There are many different methods for analyzing internal consistency, and our odd-even illustration is just one of these methods. There are several methods employing *item statistics,* which do not require that the test be split into separate halves. All that is needed for these methods is information on how each student did on every test item, but this approach generally requires electronic scoring by a computer. We must note again, however, that internal consistency methods are generally not for use with speed tests.

One last word about reliability: it is not something "possessed" by a test, like an answer sheet or a title or a scoring key. There is nothing about the test itself that has the quality "reliability," because reliablity is partly a function of *how* a test is used and on *whom* it is used. We would be more accurate in our discussion if we talked about a test yielding "reliable results" or said, "The scores on such and such a test were reliable." Technically, we can talk of a "reliable test" only when we specify the conditions under which it was administered and the sample to whom it was given.

THE STANDARD ERROR OF MEASUREMENT

When we review the results of a test, how much confidence can we place in our scores? In other words, how accurate are our scores? Suppose that individual

A made a score of 79. How much confidence do we have that our test is measuring accurately and that 79 is the individual's true score? By the *true score* we refer to the score that the test would give if there were no errors of measurement present in determining his score. We may represent this by the formula:

$$X_T = X - X_E, \text{ where}$$

X_T is the "true" score
X is the obtained score
X_E is the "error" score

It is obvious that the confidence we can place in a score depends on the gap between the obtained score and the true score. If the difference between the true and obtained scores is small, we can be quite confident that the obtained score is a good measure of the individual's performance. However, if the difference is large (i.e., there is a great discrepancy between the obtained and true scores), our test has given us a faulty measurement.

Unfortunately, our test scores are obtained scores and we have no idea of just exactly what the true score for any individual might be. But there is a way in which we can determine to a certain extent how much a score might deviate from a true value. This is commonly called the *standard error of measurement* (SEM). The formula is:

$$\text{SEM} = \text{SD} \sqrt{1 - r_t}, \text{ where}$$

SD is the standard deviation of the distribution
r_t is the reliability coefficient of the test

We use the standard error of measurement to determine the range in which the true score of an individual probably lies. If the obtained score of an individual is 75 and the standard error of measurement is 5, we can say that two out of three times his obtained score does not differ from his true score more than ±5. In two out of three times, his true score would actually fall between 70 and 80.

Let us consider an example. Suppose that the SD of a test is 10 and the reliability coefficient is .84. By the above formula the standard error of measurement is:

$$\begin{aligned} \text{SEM} &= \text{SD} \sqrt{1 - r_t} \\ &= 10 \sqrt{1 - .84} \\ &= 10 \sqrt{.16} \\ &= 10 \, (.4) \\ \text{SEM} &= 4 \end{aligned}$$

Thus the odds are two to one that the obtained score of any individual does not differ from his true score by more than ±4. If individual A had a score of 79, we can feel confident that his true score actually lies in the range from 75 to 83.

The main purpose in testing is to separate individuals in respect to the trait that we are testing. You have probably inferred by now that if two individuals score differently, this does not necessarily mean they are different in respect to the trait being measured. Suppose that one makes a score of 75 and another a score of 78 and the standard error of measurement is 4. The range for the first individual is 75 ±4, or 71 to 79, and for the second individual 78 ±4, or 74 to 82. Has our test done any separating? We cannot be sure on scores that are close together within the limits of the standard error of measurement. If there is an overlap in the range, as in this example, we cannot be sure that the true scores of the individuals are actually different. It is obvious that the smaller the standard error of measurement, the more accurate our obtained scores.

We should notice from the formula

$$\text{SEM} = \text{SD} \sqrt{1 - r_t}$$

that the reliability of the test is important in determining the size of the standard error of measurement. If r_t is perfect, or 1.0, the term under the radical reduces to zero, and the standard error of measurement is now zero. If r_t is zero, the standard error becomes the same as the SD. We can see from this that the higher the reliability of the test, the smaller the standard error of measurement.

VALIDITY

When we ask the question, "Are these test results consistent and repeatable?" we are talking about reliability. But when we ask, "Is this test testing what it is supposed to test?" we are concerned with *validity,* or the purpose of the test. Various tests may yield valid measurements of intelligence, manual dexterity, vocational interest, and a host of other traits that are amenable to measurement. Basically, we say that a test is valid if it measures what is purports to measure.

A test can be highly reliable without being valid. With a primitive IQ test which consisted of measuring the circumference of the head with a tape measure, we might get very *reliable* (i.e., consistent) measurements. However, such measurements would not be *valid* for estimating intelligence.

Test theorists have identified three basic types of validity—content validity, construct validity, and criterion-related validity. These terms all represent different ways of determining whether a test is "testing what it is supposed to test." Since the purpose of this chapter is to illustrate some of the statistical methods in test construction, we will confine our discussion to the third type, the *criterion-related* validity, because statistical analysis is a major factor in this method.

In order to determine whether a test is testing what it is supposed to test, we need to have some other measurement that is totally independent with which to compare our test. This independent "other measurement" is called the *criterion,* and the proper selection of a criterion is a vital part of criterion-related validity. The criterion must be a valid and reliable measure of what we are interested in measuring with our own test. For example, if we are constructing a new intelligence test, we would probably choose a test like the Stanford-Binet or one of the Wechsler tests as our criterion. These tests have been shown to be valid and reliable measures of intellectual ability. If our new test compares favorably with the criterion, we can say that our test is also a valid measure of intelligence.

Or let's use still another example. Suppose that we have constructed a test to predict success in college. This college entrance exam would be given to high-school seniors in the fall of their senior year. But what should we use as a criterion? What is the best indicator (most reliable and valid) of college success? The criterion most often used is the grade-point average (GPA) after the freshman year at college. We would give our test to a sample of high-school students and correlate the test results with their college grade-point averages a year later. If the correlation were high, we would be able to say that our test was a good predictor of college success, i.e., valid.

The correlational technique used most often is the familiar Pearson r. As a review of the computational techniques, let us suppose that we have constructed an arithmetic aptitude test. We have decided that as a criterion we will use one of the subtests of a well-known abilities test. The results when both tests are given to 10 pupils are shown in Table 28. Test X is our own and Test Y is the criterion.

Table 28

CALCULATION OF A VALIDITY COEFFICIENT

Pupil	Test X	Test Y	X^2	Y^2	XY
A	14	24	196	576	336
B	16	23	256	529	368
C	17	25	289	625	425
D	13	21	169	441	273
E	13	20	169	400	260
F	14	23	196	529	322
G	14	23	196	529	322
H	10	18	100	324	180
I	9	17	81	289	153
J	10	16	100	256	160
	130	210	1752	4498	2799

Calculations:

$$M_x = \frac{130}{10} = 13 \qquad M_y = \frac{210}{10} = 21$$

$$SD_x = \sqrt{\frac{\Sigma X^2}{N} - M_x^2} \qquad SD_y = \sqrt{\frac{\Sigma Y^2}{N} - M_y^2}$$

$$= \sqrt{\frac{1752}{10} - (13)^2} \qquad = \sqrt{\frac{4498}{10} - (21)^2}$$

$$= \sqrt{175.2 - 169} \qquad = \sqrt{449.8 - 441}$$

$$= \sqrt{6.2} \qquad = \sqrt{8.8}$$

$$SD_x = 2.5 \qquad SD_y = 3.0$$

Substitution:

$$r = \frac{\frac{\Sigma XY}{N} - M_x M_y}{SD_x SD_y} = \frac{\frac{2799}{10} - (13)(21)}{(2.5)(3.0)}$$

$$= \frac{279.9 - 273}{7.5} = \frac{6.9}{7.5}$$

$$r = .92$$

Since the correlation is high, we can assume that our test is measuring the same thing as the criterion. Actually, a validity coefficient of .92 is very high. Usually validity coefficients are considerably lower, with many of them in the .50 to .70 range.

Before leaving the topic of validity we must mention one important item. When we determine the validity of a test using another test as a criterion, the reliability of both tests must be high. This is logical since a validity coefficient would be meaningless if either of the tests is not reliable.

We have not made any statement on the size of a respectable validity coefficient. How large must it be before we can say that we have a valid test? The answer to this question is not a simple one—it depends on the sample taking the test and on the type of test. About all that can be said in this introductory manual is that further work with tests, additional testing courses, and practical experience will help you become sensitized to the interpretation of validity coefficients.

THE USE OF STANDARDIZED TESTS

The classroom teacher is often faced with the administration of one or more standardized tests at least once during the school year. It is usually difficult, if not impossible, for many schools to have the service of a trained test technician to handle the testing program. As a result, the administration and interpretation of the tests are left to the teacher. Some teachers begrudgingly administer the test, and, because of their feelings of inadequacy and lack of confidence in test practices, fail to make full use of the information given by the scores. On the other hand, some with a flair for testing will plunge into an intensive testing program and make all sorts of unqualified conclusions and assumptions based on the test scores.

With the present emphasis on the use of standardized tests, the teacher needs to have a middle-of-the-road approach. One has to be confident in testing and evaluation, but, at the same time, cautious and conservative in use and interpretations. This, as with anything else, is established through practice.

As was mentioned previously, a standardized test is one that has been administered to a selected sample and has had norms constructed for it on the basis of these scores. A teacher-made test is usually considered nonstandardized because it is written for the sole purpose of discrimination of achievement for one class. However, some standardized tests were at one time teacher-made tests. After much refinement, they were finally administered to a sample of students, norms were constructed, and the tests were printed and put on the market.

You will note in the preceding paragraph the repetition of the term *sample*. This forms the important first rule in the use of standardized tests: *the test that is being used should have norms based on a sample that is very much like the test group*. Otherwise, the scores made by the group will not be comparable when placed on the norms for the standardized test. The manual accompanying the test usually gives information about the nature of the sample.

Of course, many tests will not be based on a sample that is *exactly* like the group to be tested. In this case the teacher must use a certain amount of discretion in interpreting the scores. If the group to be tested is made up of pupils in a small high school in Minnesota and the test norms are based on a sample from large high schools in another state, certain allowances will have to be made.

The second rule concerns the purpose of the test. In most situations the school administration selects the test and the teacher has only the responsibility of giving the test. However, if the teacher has the freedom to select the test, *the test must be one that is going to measure what the teacher wants*. This may sound like a very low level of common sense, but the title of a test is not always indicative of its purpose. Reference should always be made to a catalog of tests that lists the information concerning the purpose of the test. If the teacher is still in doubt, most publishers offer a specimen set which contains several copies of the test, a scoring key, and instruction manual.

The third rule incorporates many smaller ones. *Follow the instruction manual carefully*. The purpose of the manual is to make the test situation as similar as possible to that of the original sample upon which the norms were based. If the norms are to be accurate, the test situations must be similar. The test manual includes instructions on how to administer the test, instructions to the examinees, time limits for the various sections of the test, and directions for plotting a profile chart of each student and the interpretation of these charts. Since each test is different, these points will not be taken up individually. However, it cannot be overemphasized that the manual must be followed carefully.

It must be remembered that standardized tests, like all others, are subject to certain limitations. Generally speaking, the standard error of measurement is usually less for standardized tests than for teacher-made tests. However, the interpretation of tests scores must take into account motivation, emotional level, and other factors that influence test scores. It can be seen that a test score is just a sample of an individual's performance. With repeated testing, the average score on these repetitions would be indicative of his performance in the long run, but a test is administered only once. His score may be too high, too low, or just right. As a result, a test score should not be considered absolute, but should be interpreted with reference to other factors.

It cannot be overemphasized that the results of a single test should be viewed with caution. Too many students have been wrongly advised against going to college, placed in the wrong ability group, etc., simply on the basis of a single test score. Cumulative records, grades, confidential reports, and other test results should be interpreted as a meaningful whole. Attaching too much importance to a single test score is the mark of a novice.

PROBLEMS

1. A world geography quiz was given to 10 high-school freshmen. Each student's score was separated to give the number of odd and even items correct. Calculate the reliability of this test.

Student	X (Odd)	Y (Even)	X^2	Y^2	XY
A	16	14			
B	14	12			
C	14	13			
D	13	15			
E	13	16			
F	12	12			
G	10	9			
H	10	8			
I	9	7			
J	9	4			

a. $M_x =$ $M_y =$

   $SD_x =$ $SD_y =$

$$r_{oe} = \frac{\frac{\Sigma XY}{N} - M_x M_y}{SD_x SD_y} =$$

$$r_t = \frac{2r_{oe}}{1 + r_{oe}} =$$

b. Is this test reliable?

2. A school psychologist constructs a test to measure vocabulary proficiency in third-graders and would like to know how her test compares with the vocabulary subtest of a well-known IQ test. She gives both tests to 10 third-graders. Calculate a validity coefficient, using the Pearson r.

Pupil	X (Hers)	Y (IQ)	X^2	Y^2	XY
A	23	16			
B	22	17			
C	20	15			
D	19	16			
E	19	10			
F	18	12			
G	17	9			
H	17	9			
I	13	8			
J	12	8			

a. $M_x =$　　　　　　　　　$M_y =$

$SD_x =$　　　　　　　　　$SD_y =$

$$r = \frac{\frac{\Sigma XY}{N} - M_x M_y}{SD_x SD_y} =$$

b. Do the results of her test agree with the IQ subtest?

Evaluation and Interpretation of Tests

3. Fifteen seventh-graders are given a mathematics achievement test. Each student's score was separated to give the number of odd and even items correct. Calculate the reliability of this test.

Student	X (Odd)	Y (Even)	X^2	Y^2	XY
A	12	13			
B	15	14			
C	13	14			
D	11	12			
E	11	11			
F	9	8			
G	8	8			
H	8	9			
I	9	10			
J	8	9			
K	4	4			
L	7	8			
M	10	11			
N	4	7			
O	6	12			

a. $M_X =$ $M_Y =$

$SD_x =$ $SD_y =$

$$r_{oe} = \frac{\frac{\Sigma XY}{N} - M_x M_y}{SD_x SD_y} =$$

$$r_t = \frac{2r_{oe}}{1 + r_{oe}}$$

b. Is this test consistent in its results?

Evaluation and Interpretation of Tests

4. A guidance counselor constructs a college entrance exam which he hopes will predict college success. He administers his exam to 15 college-bound high-school seniors and, one year later, he tabulates their college GPAs. Calculate a validity coefficient between the test scores (X) and the GPAs (Y).

Student	X	Y	X^2	Y^2	XY
A	22	3.2			
B	21	3.0			
C	20	3.2			
D	18	3.2			
E	17	2.8			
F	16	2.8			
G	16	2.9			
H	16	2.7			
I	16	2.8			
J	15	2.8			
K	14	2.7			
L	14	2.4			
M	13	2.6			
N	11	2.6			
O	11	2.3			

a. $M_x =$ $\qquad$ $M_y =$

Evaluation and Interpretation of Tests 115

$SD_x =$ $SD_y =$

$$r = \frac{\frac{\Sigma XY}{N} - M_x M_y}{SD_x SD_y} =$$

b. Does this validity coefficient indicate that the exam is successful in predicting college success?

5. The reliability of an aptitude test that we are using is .91, and the SD of the test is 8.5. If John has an observed score of 47, we could say that chances are two out of three that his *true* score lies between

_____ and _____ .

Appendix I

ANSWERS TO PROBLEMS

CHAPTER 3

1. a. M = 260/20 = 13
2. a. M = 460/20 = 23; Median = 24.5; Mode = 28
   b. The mode is the poorest because the score made most frequently falls at the extreme end of the distribution.
3. M = 267/15 = 17.8; Median = 17; Mode = 17
4. M = 50.65; Median = 50.3; Mode = 49
5. a. M = 43.79; Median = 45.93; Mode = 54.5
   c. Negative skewness
   d. With the large number of high scores, it is evident that the test was too easy for this group.

CHAPTER 4

1. Below average. His score is comparable to that of someone just entering the third grade.
2. Very likely due to superior mastery of material at her own age level—not of the more advanced concepts.
3. P_{36} = 20; PR = 72
4. a. P_{30} = 33.35
   b. P_{64} = 47.18
   c. P_{90} = 60.93
5. a. P_{50} = 69.5
   b. P_{90} = 78.67
   c. P_{22} = 63.25

CHAPTER 5

1. a. SD = $\sqrt{46.5/10}$ = 2.16
   b. SD = $\sqrt{(609/10) - (7.5)^2}$ = 2.16
   c. The whole score method would probably be easier because the deviation method requires both subtracting and squaring.

2. $SD = \sqrt{6.93} = 2.63$
3. a. $z = 2$ for algebra vs. $z = 1.6$ for English
   b. Algebra, $T = 70$; English, $T = 66$
   c. $z = -1.0$; $T = 40$
4. a. $M = 200/20 = 10$; Median $= 11$; Mode $= 11$; $SD = \sqrt{8.30} = 2.88$
   b. $M \pm 1\ SD = 10 \pm 2.88$, or 7.12 to 12.88
5. $M = 450/30 = 15$; Median $= 15$; Mode $= 15$; $SD = \sqrt{26.47} = 5.14$
6. $M = 32.4$; $SD = 5\sqrt{3.35} = 5(1.83) = 9.15$
7. $M = 14.5$; Median $= 14.5$; Mode $= 15$; $SD = 3\sqrt{2.36} = 3(1.54) = 4.62$

CHAPTER 6

1. a. $r_s = 1 - \dfrac{6(26)}{10(100-1)} = 1 - \dfrac{156}{990} = 1 - .16 = .84$

   b. There appears to be a high degree of relationship, because a coefficient of .84 would indicate that those who scored high on one test scored high on the other, and those that scored low on one scored low on the other.

2. a. $r_s = 1 - \dfrac{6(132)}{10(100-1)} = 1 - \dfrac{792}{990} = 1 - .80 = .20$

   b. With a coefficient as low as .20 it would appear that there is no relationship between gymnastic and wrestling ability.

3. a. $M_x = 10$; $M_y = 16$
   b. $SD_x = \sqrt{11.6} = 3.41$; $SD_y = \sqrt{13.8} = 3.71$
   c. $r = \dfrac{\dfrac{1707}{10} - (10)(16)}{(3.41)(3.71)} = .85$

   d. Yes, a coefficient of .85 shows that the relationship is very good.

4. a. $M_x = 9$; $M_y = 8$
   b. $SD_x = \sqrt{6.8} = 2.61$; $SD_y = \sqrt{17.4} = 4.17$
   c. $r = \dfrac{\dfrac{622}{10} - (9)(8)}{(2.61)(4.17)} = -.90$

   d. It is doubtful that such a large negative coefficient would be obtained in actual practice. However, in this fictitious example, it would indicate that ability in music history would be accompanied by a lack of ability in automotive mechanics!

5. These two tests appear to be measuring the same skill, since those that have high scores on one have high scores on the other. The actual coefficient for these data is .90.

Appendix I: Answers to Problems

CHAPTER 7

1. a. $M_x = 12; M_y = 11; SD_x = \sqrt{5.2} = 2.28; SD_y = \sqrt{13.4} = 3.66$

   $$r_{oe} = \frac{\frac{1390}{10} - (12)(11)}{(2.28)(3.66)} = .84; \quad r_t = \frac{2(.84)}{1 + .84} = .91$$

   b. With an r_t of .91, this test gives consistent results.

2. a. $M_x = 18; M_y = 12; SD_x = \sqrt{11} = 3.32; SD_y = \sqrt{12} = 3.46$

   $$r = \frac{\frac{2258}{10} - (18)(12)}{(3.32)(3.46)} = .85$$

   b. With a validity coefficient this high, the results of both tests agree very well, and both tests appear to be measuring the same thing.

3. a. $M_x = 9; M_y = 10; SD_x = \sqrt{9.07} = 3.01; SD_y = \sqrt{7.33} = 2.71$

   $$r_{oe} = \frac{\frac{1453}{15} - (9)(10)}{(3.01)(2.71)} = .84; \quad r_t = \frac{2(.84)}{1 + .84} = .91$$

   b. Yes, an r_t of .91 indicates great consistency.

4. a. $M_x = 16; M_y = 2.8; SD_x = \sqrt{10} = 3.16; SD_y = \sqrt{.07} = .26$

   $$r = \frac{\frac{682.9}{15} - (16)(2.8)}{(3.16)(.26)} = .89$$

   b. With a validity coefficient this high, the homemade entrance exam is predicting GPA very well.

5. SEM = $8.5\sqrt{1 - .91} = 8.5\sqrt{.09} = 8.5(.3) = 2.55$; 47 ±2.55, or 44.45 to 49.55.

Appendix II

TABLE OF SQUARES AND SQUARE ROOTS

OF NUMBERS FROM 1 to 1000*

N	N^2	$\sqrt{N}$	N	N^2	$\sqrt{N}$	N	N^2	$\sqrt{N}$
1	1	1.0000	41	1681	6.4031	81	6561	9.0000
2	4	1.4142	42	1764	6.4807	82	6724	9.0554
3	9	1.7321	43	1849	6.5574	83	6889	9.1104
4	16	2.0000	44	1936	6.6332	84	7056	9.1652
5	25	2.2361	45	2025	6.7082	85	7225	9.2195
6	36	2.4495	46	2116	6.7823	86	7396	9.2736
7	49	2.6458	47	2209	6.8557	87	7569	9.3274
8	64	2.8284	48	2304	6.9282	88	7744	9.3808
9	81	3.0000	49	2401	7.0000	89	7921	9.4340
10	100	3.1623	50	2500	7.0711	90	8100	9.4868
11	121	3.3166	51	2601	7.1414	91	8281	9.5394
12	144	3.4641	52	2704	7.2111	92	8464	9.5917
13	169	3.6056	53	2809	7.2801	93	8649	9.6437
14	196	3.7417	54	2916	7.3485	94	8836	9.6954
15	225	3.8730	55	3025	7.4162	95	9025	9.7468
16	256	4.0000	56	3136	7.4833	96	9216	9.7980
17	289	4.1231	57	3249	7.5498	97	9409	9.8489
18	324	4.2426	58	3364	7.6158	98	9604	9.8995
19	361	4.3589	59	3481	7.6811	99	9801	9.9499
20	400	4.4721	60	3600	7.7460	100	10000	10.0000
21	441	4.5826	61	3721	7.8102	101	10201	10.0499
22	484	4.6904	62	3844	7.8740	102	10404	10.0995
23	529	4.7958	63	3969	7.9373	103	10609	10.1489
24	576	4.8990	64	4096	8.0000	104	10816	10.1980
25	625	5.0000	65	4225	8.0623	105	11025	10.2470
26	676	5.0990	66	4356	8.1240	106	11236	10.2956
27	729	5.1962	67	4489	8.1854	107	11449	10.3441
28	784	5.2915	68	4624	8.2462	108	11664	10.3923
29	841	5.3852	69	4761	8.3066	109	11881	10.4403
30	900	5.4772	70	4900	8.3666	110	12100	10.4881
31	961	5.5678	71	5041	8.4261	111	12321	10.5357
32	1024	5.6569	72	5184	8.4853	112	12544	10.5830
33	1089	5.7446	73	5329	8.5440	113	12769	10.6301
34	1156	5.8310	74	5476	8.6023	114	12996	10.6771
35	1225	5.9161	75	5625	8.6603	115	13225	10.7238
36	1296	6.0000	76	5776	8.7178	116	13456	10.7703
37	1369	6.0828	77	5929	8.7750	117	13689	10.8167
38	1444	6.1644	78	6084	8.8318	118	13924	10.8628
39	1521	6.2450	79	6241	8.8882	119	14161	10.9087
40	1600	6.3246	80	6400	8.9443	120	14400	10.9545

*Portions of this table have been reproduced from J. W. Dunlap and A. K. Kurtz, *Handbook of Statistical Nomographs, Tables and Formulas,* World Book Company, New York (1932) by permission of the authors and publishers.

Appendix II: Table of Squares and Square Roots

N	N^2	$\sqrt{N}$	N	N^2	$\sqrt{N}$	N	N^2	$\sqrt{N}$
121	14641	11.0000	161	25921	12.6886	201	40401	14.1774
122	14884	11.0454	162	26244	12.7279	202	40804	14.2127
123	15129	11.0905	163	26569	12.7671	203	41209	14.2478
124	15376	11.1355	164	26896	12.8062	204	41616	14.2829
125	15625	11.1803	165	27225	12.8452	205	42025	14.3178
126	15876	11.2250	166	27556	12.8841	206	42436	14.3527
127	16129	11.2694	167	27889	12.9228	207	42849	14.3875
128	16384	11.3137	168	28224	12.9615	208	43264	14.4222
129	16641	11.3578	169	28561	13.0000	209	43681	14.4568
130	16900	11.4018	170	28900	13.0384	210	44100	14.4914
131	17161	11.4455	171	29241	13.0767	211	44521	14.5258
132	17424	11.4891	172	29584	13.1149	212	44944	14.5602
133	17689	11.5326	173	29929	13.1529	213	45369	14.5945
134	17956	11.5758	174	30276	13.1909	214	45796	14.6287
135	18225	11.6190	175	30625	13.2288	215	46225	14.6629
136	18496	11.6619	176	30976	13.2665	216	46656	14.6969
137	18769	11.7047	177	31329	13.3041	217	47089	14.7309
138	19044	11.7473	178	31684	13.3417	218	47524	14.7648
139	19321	11.7898	179	32041	13.3791	219	47961	14.7986
140	19600	11.8322	180	32400	13.4164	220	48400	14.8324
141	19881	11.8743	181	32761	13.4536	221	48841	14.8661
142	20164	11.9164	182	33124	13.4907	222	49284	14.8997
143	20449	11.9583	183	33489	13.5277	223	49729	14.9332
144	20736	12.0000	184	33856	13.5647	224	50176	14.9666
145	21025	12.0416	185	34225	13.6015	225	50625	15.0000
146	21316	12.0830	186	34596	13.6382	226	51076	15.0333
147	21609	12.1244	187	34969	13.6748	227	51529	15.0665
148	21904	12.1655	188	35344	13.7113	228	51984	15.0997
149	22201	12.2066	189	35721	13.7477	229	52441	15.1327
150	22500	12.2474	190	36100	13.7840	230	52900	15.1658
151	22801	12.2882	191	36481	13.8203	231	53361	15.1987
152	23104	12.3288	192	36864	13.8564	232	53824	15.2315
153	23409	12.3693	193	37249	13.8924	233	54289	15.2643
154	23716	12.4097	194	37636	13.9284	234	54756	15.2971
155	24025	12.4499	195	38025	13.9642	235	55225	15.3297
156	24336	12.4900	196	38416	14.0000	236	55696	15.3623
157	24649	12.5300	197	38809	14.0357	237	56169	15.3948
158	24964	12.5698	198	39204	14.0712	238	56644	15.4272
159	25281	12.6095	199	39601	14.1067	239	57121	15.4596
160	25600	12.6491	200	40000	14.1421	240	57600	15.4919

Appendix II: Table of Squares and Square Roots

N	N^2	$\sqrt{N}$	N	N^2	$\sqrt{N}$	N	N^2	$\sqrt{N}$
241	58081	15.5242	281	78961	16.7631	321	103041	17.9165
242	58564	15.5563	282	79524	16.7929	322	103684	17.9444
243	59049	15.5885	283	80089	16.8226	323	104329	17.9722
244	59536	15.6205	284	80656	16.8523	324	104976	18.0000
245	60025	15.6525	285	81225	16.8819	325	105625	18.0278
246	60516	15.6844	286	81796	16.9115	326	106276	18.0555
247	61009	15.7162	287	82369	16.9411	327	106929	18.0831
248	61504	15.7480	288	82944	16.9706	328	107584	18.1108
249	62001	15.7797	289	83521	17.0000	329	108241	18.1384
250	62500	15.8114	290	84100	17.0294	330	108900	18.1659
251	63001	15.8430	291	84681	17.0587	331	109561	18.1934
252	63504	15.8745	292	85264	17.0880	332	110224	18.2209
253	64009	15.9060	293	85849	17.1172	333	110889	18.2483
254	64516	15.9374	294	86436	17.1464	334	111556	18.2757
255	65025	15.9687	295	87025	17.1756	335	112225	18.3030
256	65536	16.0000	296	87616	17.2047	336	112896	18.3303
257	66049	16.0312	297	88209	17.2337	337	113569	18.3576
258	66564	16.0624	298	88804	17.2627	338	114244	18.3848
259	67081	16.0935	299	89401	17.2916	339	114921	18.4120
260	67600	16.1245	300	90000	17.3205	340	115600	18.4391
261	68121	16.1555	301	90601	17.3494	341	116281	18.4662
262	68644	16.1864	302	91204	17.3781	342	116964	18.4932
263	69169	16.2173	303	91809	17.4069	343	117649	18.5203
264	69696	16.2481	304	92416	17.4356	344	118336	18.5472
265	70225	16.2788	305	93025	17.4642	345	119025	18.5742
266	70756	16.3095	306	93636	17.4929	346	119716	18.6011
267	71289	16.3401	307	94249	17.5214	347	120409	18.6279
268	71824	16.3707	308	94864	17.5499	348	121104	18.6548
269	72361	16.4012	309	95481	17.5784	349	121801	18.6815
270	72900	16.4317	310	96100	17.6068	350	122500	18.7083
271	73441	16.4621	311	96721	17.6352	351	123201	18.7350
272	73984	16.4924	312	97344	17.6635	352	123904	18.7617
273	74529	16.5227	313	97969	17.6918	353	124609	18.7883
274	75076	16.5529	314	98596	17.7200	354	125316	18.8149
275	75625	16.5831	315	99225	17.7482	355	126025	18.8414
276	76176	16.6132	316	99856	17.7764	356	126736	18.8680
277	76729	16.6433	317	100489	17.8045	357	127449	18.8944
278	77284	16.6733	318	101124	17.8326	358	128164	18.9209
279	77841	16.7033	319	101761	17.8606	359	128881	18.9473
280	78400	16.7332	320	102400	17.8885	360	129600	18.9737

Appendix II: Table of Squares and Square Roots

N	N²	√N	N	N²	√N	N	N²	√N
361	130321	19.0000	401	160801	20.0250	441	194481	21.0000
362	131044	19.0263	402	161604	20.0499	442	195364	21.0238
363	131769	19.0526	403	162409	20.0749	443	196249	21.0476
364	132496	19.0788	404	163216	20.0998	444	197136	21.0713
365	133225	19.1050	405	164025	20.1246	445	198025	21.0950
366	133956	19.1311	406	164836	20.1494	446	198916	21.1187
367	134689	19.1572	407	165649	20.1742	447	199809	21.1424
368	135424	19.1833	408	166464	20.1990	448	200704	21.1660
369	136161	19.2094	409	167281	20.2237	449	201601	21.1896
370	136900	19.2354	410	168100	20.2485	450	202500	21.2132
371	137641	19.2614	411	168921	20.2731	451	203401	21.2368
372	138384	19.2873	412	169744	20.2978	452	204304	21.2603
373	139129	19.3132	413	170569	20.3224	453	205209	21.2838
374	139876	19.3391	414	171396	20.3470	454	206116	21.3073
375	140625	19.3649	415	172225	20.3715	455	207025	21.3307
376	141376	19.3907	416	173056	20.3961	456	207936	21.3542
377	142129	19.4165	417	173889	20.4206	457	208849	21.3776
378	142884	19.4422	418	174724	20.4450	458	209764	21.4009
379	143641	19.4679	419	175561	20.4695	459	210681	21.4243
380	144400	19.4936	420	176400	20.4939	460	211600	21.4476
381	145161	19.5192	421	177241	20.5183	461	212521	21.4709
382	145924	19.5448	422	178084	20.5426	462	213444	21.4942
383	146689	19.5704	423	178929	20.5670	463	214369	21.5174
384	147456	19.5959	424	179776	20.5913	464	215296	21.5407
385	148225	19.6214	425	180625	20.6155	465	216225	21.5639
386	148996	19.6469	426	181476	20.6398	466	217156	21.5870
387	149769	19.6723	427	182329	20.6640	467	218089	21.6102
388	150544	19.6977	428	183184	20.6882	468	219024	21.6333
389	151321	19.7231	429	184041	20.7123	469	219961	21.6564
390	152100	19.7484	430	184900	20.7364	470	220900	21.6795
391	152881	19.7737	431	185761	20.7605	471	221841	21.7025
392	153664	19.7990	432	186624	20.7846	472	222784	21.7256
393	154449	19.8242	433	187489	20.8087	473	223729	21.7486
394	155236	19.8494	434	188356	20.8327	474	224676	21.7715
395	156025	19.8746	435	189225	20.8567	475	225625	21.7945
396	156816	19.8997	436	190096	20.8806	476	226576	21.8174
397	157609	19.9249	437	190969	20.9045	477	227529	21.8403
398	158404	19.9499	438	191844	20.9284	478	228484	21.8632
399	159201	19.9750	439	192721	20.9523	479	229441	21.8861
400	160000	20.0000	440	193600	20.9762	480	230400	21.9089

Appendix II: Table of Squares and Square Roots

N	N^2	$\sqrt{N}$	N	N^2	$\sqrt{N}$	N	N^2	$\sqrt{N}$
481	231361	21.9317	521	271441	22.8254	561	314721	23.6854
482	232324	21.9545	522	272484	22.8473	562	315844	23.7065
483	233289	21.9773	523	273529	22.8692	563	316969	23.7276
484	234256	22.0000	524	274576	22.8910	564	318096	23.7487
485	235225	22.0227	525	275625	22.9129	565	319225	23.7697
486	236196	22.0454	526	276676	22.9347	566	320356	23.7908
487	237169	22.0681	527	277729	22.9565	567	321489	23.8118
488	238144	22.0907	528	278784	22.9783	568	322624	23.8328
489	239121	22.1133	529	279841	23.0000	569	323761	23.8537
490	240100	22.1359	530	280900	23.0217	570	324900	23.8747
491	241081	22.1585	531	281961	23.0434	571	326041	23.8956
492	242064	22.1811	532	283024	23.0651	572	327184	23.9165
493	243049	22.2036	533	284089	23.0868	573	328329	23.9374
494	244036	22.2261	534	285156	23.1084	574	329476	23.9583
495	245025	22.2486	535	286225	23.1301	575	330625	23.9792
496	246016	22.2711	536	287296	23.1517	576	331776	24.0000
497	247009	22.2935	537	288369	23.1733	577	332929	24.0208
498	248004	22.3159	538	289444	23.1948	578	334084	24.0416
499	249001	22.3383	539	290521	23.2164	579	335241	24.0624
500	250000	22.3607	540	291600	23.2379	580	336400	24.0832
501	251001	22.3830	541	292681	23.2594	581	337561	24.1039
502	252004	22.4054	542	293764	23.2809	582	338724	24.1247
503	253009	22.4277	543	294849	23.3024	583	339889	24.1454
504	254016	22.4499	544	295936	23.3238	584	341056	24.1661
505	255025	22.4722	545	297025	23.3452	585	342225	24.1868
506	256036	22.4944	546	298116	23.3666	586	343396	24.2074
507	257049	22.5167	547	299209	23.3880	587	344569	24.2281
508	258064	22.5389	548	300304	23.4094	588	345744	24.2487
509	259081	22.5610	549	301401	23.4307	589	346921	24.2693
510	260100	22.5832	550	302500	23.4521	590	348100	24.2899
511	261121	22.6053	551	303601	23.4734	591	349281	24.3105
512	262144	22.6274	552	304704	23.4947	592	350464	24.3311
513	263169	22.6495	553	305809	23.5160	593	351649	24.3516
514	264196	22.6716	554	306916	23.5372	594	352836	24.3721
515	265225	22.6936	555	308025	23.5584	595	354025	24.3926
516	266256	22.7156	556	309136	23.5797	596	355216	24.4131
517	267289	22.7376	557	310249	23.6008	597	356409	24.4336
518	268324	22.7596	558	311364	23.6220	598	357604	24.4540
519	269361	22.7816	559	312481	23.6432	599	358801	24.4745
520	270400	22.8035	560	313600	23.6643	600	360000	24.4949

Appendix II: Table of Squares and Square Roots

N	N²	√N	N	N²	√N	N	N²	√N
601	361201	24.5153	641	410881	25.3180	681	463761	26.0960
602	362404	24.5357	642	412164	25.3377	682	465124	26.1151
603	363609	24.5561	643	413449	25.3574	683	466489	26.1343
604	364816	24.5764	644	414736	25.3772	684	467856	26.1534
605	366025	24.5967	645	416025	25.3969	685	469225	26.1725
606	367236	24.6171	646	417316	25.4165	686	470596	26.1916
607	368449	24.6374	647	418609	25.4362	687	471969	26.2107
608	369664	24.6577	648	419904	25.4558	688	473344	26.2298
609	370881	24.6779	649	421201	25.4755	689	474721	26.2488
610	372100	24.6982	650	422500	25.4951	690	476100	26.2679
611	373321	24.7184	651	423801	25.5147	691	477481	26.2869
612	374544	24.7386	652	425104	25.5343	692	478864	26.3059
613	375769	24.7588	653	426409	25.5539	693	480249	26.3249
614	376996	24.7790	654	427716	25.5734	694	481636	26.3439
615	378225	24.7992	655	429025	25.5930	695	483025	26.3629
616	379456	24.8193	656	430336	25.6125	696	484416	26.3818
617	380689	24.8395	657	431649	25.6320	697	485809	26.4008
618	381924	24.8596	658	432964	25.6515	698	487204	26.4197
619	383161	24.8797	659	434281	25.6710	699	488601	26.4386
620	384400	24.8998	660	435600	25.6905	700	490000	26.4575
621	385641	24.9199	661	436921	25.7099	701	491401	26.4764
622	386884	24.9399	662	438244	25.7294	702	492804	26.4953
623	388129	24.9600	663	439569	25.7488	703	494209	26.5141
624	389376	24.9800	664	440896	25.7682	704	495616	26.5330
625	390625	25.0000	665	442225	25.7876	705	497025	26.5518
626	391876	25.0200	666	443556	25.8070	706	498436	26.5707
627	393129	25.0400	667	444889	25.8263	707	499849	26.5895
628	394384	25.0599	668	446224	25.8457	708	501264	26.6083
629	395641	25.0799	669	447561	25.8650	709	502681	26.6271
630	396900	25.0998	670	448900	25.8844	710	504100	26.6458
631	398161	25.1197	671	450241	25.9037	711	505521	26.6646
632	399424	25.1396	672	451584	25.9230	712	506944	26.6833
633	400689	25.1595	673	452929	25.9422	713	508369	26.7021
634	401956	25.1794	674	454276	25.9615	714	509796	26.7208
635	403225	25.1992	675	455625	25.9808	715	511225	26.7395
636	404496	25.2190	676	456976	26.0000	716	512656	26.7582
637	405769	25.2389	677	458329	26.0192	717	514089	26.7769
638	407044	25.2587	678	459684	26.0384	718	515524	26.7955
639	408321	25.2784	679	461041	26.0576	719	516961	26.8142
640	409600	25.2982	680	462400	26.0768	720	518400	26.8328

Appendix II: Table of Squares and Square Roots

N	N^2	$\sqrt{N}$	N	N^2	$\sqrt{N}$	N	N^2	$\sqrt{N}$
721	519841	26.8514	761	579121	27.5862	801	641601	28.3019
722	521284	26.8701	762	580644	27.6043	802	643204	28.3196
723	522729	26.8887	763	582169	27.6225	803	644809	28.3373
724	524176	26.9072	764	583696	27.6405	804	646416	28.3549
725	525625	26.9258	765	585225	27.6586	805	648025	28.3725
726	527076	26.9444	766	586756	27.6767	806	649636	28.3901
727	528529	26.9629	767	588289	27.6948	807	651249	28.4077
728	529984	26.9815	768	589824	27.7128	808	652864	28.4253
729	531441	27.0000	769	591361	27.7308	809	654481	28.4429
730	532900	27.0185	770	592900	27.7489	810	656100	28.4605
731	534361	27.0370	771	594441	27.7669	811	657721	28.4781
732	535824	27.0555	772	595984	27.7849	812	659344	28.4956
733	537289	27.0740	773	597529	27.8029	813	660969	28.5132
734	538756	27.0924	774	599076	27.8209	814	662596	28.5307
735	540225	27.1109	775	600625	27.8388	815	664225	28.5482
736	541696	27.1293	776	602176	27.8568	816	665856	28.5657
737	543169	27.1477	777	603729	27.8747	817	667489	28.5832
738	544644	27.1662	778	605284	27.8927	818	669124	28.6007
739	546121	27.1846	779	606841	27.9106	819	670761	28.6182
740	547600	27.2029	780	608400	27.9285	820	672400	28.6356
741	549081	27.2213	781	609961	27.9464	821	674041	28.6531
742	550564	27.2397	782	611524	27.9643	822	675684	28.6705
743	552049	27.2580	783	613089	27.9821	823	677329	28.6880
744	553536	27.2764	784	614656	28.0000	824	678976	28.7054
745	555025	27.2947	785	616225	28.0179	825	680625	28.7228
746	556516	27.3130	786	617796	28.0357	826	682276	28.7402
747	558009	27.3313	787	619369	28.0535	827	683929	28.7576
748	559504	27.3496	788	620944	28.0713	828	685584	28.7750
749	561001	27.3679	789	622521	28.0891	829	687241	28.7924
750	562500	27.3861	790	624100	28.1069	830	688900	28.8097
751	564001	27.4044	791	625681	28.1247	831	690561	28.8271
752	565504	27.4226	792	627264	28.1425	832	692224	28.8444
753	567009	27.4408	793	628849	28.1603	833	693889	28.8617
754	568516	27.4591	794	630436	28.1780	834	695556	28.8791
755	570025	27.4773	795	632025	28.1957	835	697225	28.8964
756	571536	27.4955	796	633616	28.2135	836	698896	28.9137
757	573049	27.5136	797	635209	28.2312	837	700569	28.9310
758	574564	27.5318	798	636804	28.2489	838	702244	28.9482
759	576081	27.5500	799	638401	28.2666	839	703921	28.9655
760	577600	27.5681	800	640000	28.2843	840	705600	28.9828

Appendix II: Table of Squares and Square Roots

N	N^2	$\sqrt{N}$	N	N^2	$\sqrt{N}$	N	N^2	$\sqrt{N}$
841	707281	29.0000	881	776161	29.6816	921	848241	30.3480
842	708964	29.0172	882	777924	29.6985	922	850084	30.3645
843	710649	29.0345	883	779689	29.7153	923	851929	30.3809
844	712336	29.0517	884	781456	29.7321	924	853776	30.3974
845	714025	29.0689	885	783225	29.7489	925	855625	30.4138
846	715716	29.0861	886	784996	29.7658	926	857476	30.4302
847	717409	29.1033	887	786769	29.7825	927	859329	30.4467
848	719104	29.1204	888	788544	29.7993	928	861184	30.4631
849	720801	29.1376	889	790321	29.8161	929	863041	30.4795
850	722500	29.1548	890	792100	29.8329	930	864900	30.4959
851	724201	29.1719	891	793881	29.8496	931	866761	30.5123
852	725904	29.1890	892	795664	29.8664	932	868624	30.5287
853	727609	29.2062	893	797449	29.8831	933	870489	30.5450
854	729316	29.2233	894	799236	29.8998	934	872356	30.5614
855	731025	29.2404	895	801025	29.9166	935	874225	30.5778
856	732736	29.2575	896	802816	29.9333	936	876096	30.5941
857	734449	29.2746	897	804609	29.9500	937	877969	30.6105
858	736164	29.2916	898	806404	29.9666	938	879844	30.6268
859	737881	29.3087	899	808201	29.9833	939	881721	30.6431
860	739600	29.3258	900	810000	30.0000	940	883600	30.6594
861	741321	29.3428	901	811801	30.0167	941	885481	30.6757
862	743044	29.3598	902	813604	30.0333	942	887364	30.6920
863	744769	29.3769	903	815409	30.0500	943	889249	30.7083
864	746496	29.3939	904	817216	30.0666	944	891136	30.7246
865	748225	29.4109	905	819025	30.0832	945	893025	30.7409
866	749956	29.4279	906	820836	30.0998	946	894916	30.7571
867	751689	29.4449	907	822649	30.1164	947	896809	30.7734
868	753424	29.4618	908	824464	30.1330	948	898704	30.7896
869	755161	29.4788	909	826281	30.1496	949	900601	30.8058
870	756900	29.4958	910	828100	30.1662	950	902500	30.8221
871	758641	29.5127	911	829921	30.1828	951	904401	30.8383
872	760384	29.5296	912	831744	30.1993	952	906304	30.8545
873	762129	29.5466	913	833569	30.2159	953	908209	30.8707
874	763876	29.5635	914	835396	30.2324	954	910116	30.8869
875	765625	29.5804	915	837225	30.2490	955	912025	30.9031
876	767376	29.5973	916	839056	30.2655	956	913936	30.9192
877	769129	29.6142	917	840889	30.2820	957	915849	30.9354
878	770884	29.6311	918	842724	30.2985	958	917764	30.9516
879	772641	29.6479	919	844561	30.3150	959	919681	30.9677
880	774400	29.6648	920	846400	30.3315	960	921600	30.9839

N	N^2	$\sqrt{N}$
961	923521	31.0000
962	925444	31.0161
963	927369	31.0322
964	929296	31.0483
965	931225	31.0644
966	933156	31.0805
967	935089	31.0966
968	937024	31.1127
969	938961	31.1288
970	940900	31.1448
971	942841	31.1609
972	944784	31.1769
973	946729	31.1929
974	948676	31.2090
975	950625	31.2250
976	952576	31.2410
977	954529	31.2570
978	956484	31.2730
979	958441	31.2890
980	960400	31.3050
981	962361	31.3209
982	964324	31.3369
983	966289	31.3528
984	968256	31.3688
985	970225	31.3847
986	972196	31.4006
987	974169	31.4166
988	976144	31.4325
989	978121	31.4484
990	980100	31.4643
991	982081	31.4802
992	984064	31.4960
993	986049	31.5119
994	988036	31.5278
995	990025	31.5436
996	992016	31.5595
997	994009	31.5753
998	996004	31.5911
999	998001	31.6070
1000	1000000	31.6228

INDEX

Age-grade norms, 49-51
Alternate forms, *see* Parallel forms method
Average, 27, 33. *See also* Mean

Bar graph, 9
Bimodal distribution, 30

Central tendency, 27
Coefficient of correlation, 80-83, 97
Comparable forms, *see* Parallel forms method
Consistency, 97
Construct validity, 104
Content validity, 104
Correlation, 79-88
Correlation coefficient, 80-83, 97
Criterion-related validity, 104-106
Crude mode, 38-39
Curve, normal, 10-11, 63, 65-68
Curve, skewed, 12-15, 33-34

Deviation score, 28-29
Distribution, bimodal, 30
Distribution, frequency, 5-8

Frequency distribution, 5-8
Frequency polygon, 10-11

Graph bar, 9
Graphing, 7, 9-11
Grouped data, 6-8
Grouped data, calculations from, 34-39, 52-54, 69-70, 88

Histogram, 9-10

Internal consistency methods, 99-102
Interval scale, 2
Item statistics, 102

Mean, 27-29, 32-34, 35-37
Measurement, 1
Median, 31-34, 37-38
Mode, 30, 32-34, 38-39
Mode, crude, 38-39

Negative skewness, 12-15, 33
Nominal scale, 1-2
Normal curve, 10-12, 63, 65-68
Norms, 49-54
Norms, age-grade, 49-51
Norms, percentile, 51-52

Odd-even method, 99-102
Ordinal scale, 2

Parallel forms method, 98-99, 102
Pearson r, 85-88
Percentile norms, 51-52
Percentile ranks, 51
Percentiles, 51-54
Perfect negative correlation, 80
Perfect positive correlation, 79-80
Polygon, frequency, 10-11
Positive skewness, 12-15, 34
Product-moment method, 85-88

Range, 59-60
Rank-difference method, 83-85, 87-88
Ratio scale, 2
Raw score, 28-29
Relationship of two variables, 79
Reliability, 97-102

Sampling, 107
Scale, interval, 2
Scale, nominal, 1-2
Scale, ordinal, 2
Scale, ratio, 2
Scales, types of, 1-3
Scattergram, 81-82
Score, deviation, 28-29
Score, raw, 28-29
Score, T, 67-68
Score, true, 103-104
Score, z, 66-68
Simple frequency distribution, 7-8
Skewness, 12-15, 33-34
Spearman-Brown prophecy formula, 99-101
Spearman rho, 83-85, 87-88

Speed tests, 101, 102
Split-half method, 101, 102
Standard deviation, 60-70
Standard error of measurement, 103-104
Standardized tests, 106-108

T score, 67-68
Test-retest method, 98, 102
True score, 103-104

Ungrouped data, 28

Validity, 104-106
Variability, 59-68

z score, 66-68